VIKINGS

LEGENDARY WARRIORS OF LAND AND SEA

CENTENNIAL BOOKS

VIKINGS

LEGENDARY WARRIORS OF LAND AND SEA

ROBERT EDELSTEIN
KELLY FARRELL

CENTENNIAL BOOKS

CONTENTS

32

52

24

114

WARRIORS
OF LAND AND SEA

THE VIKINGS FORGED A RICH, COMPLICATED LEGACY THAT REMAINS PUZZLING AND EVER-PRESENT.

For the Vikings of lore, life was all about the quest.

Fearless and efficient, determined and destructive, single-minded and strategic of purpose, the legendary Scandinavian warriors first sailed to the British Isles at the end of the eighth century, with plunder on their minds. Arriving in stealth in their slender but terrifying longships, they attacked with a kind of shock and awe their victims could never have imagined possible.

For three centuries during the Middle Ages, the Vikings assaulted and ruled some of the wealthiest cities on the globe, keeping the Europeans under their thumbs. The most terrifying Vikings were, as they called themselves, "berserkers" who would one day be the center of sagas—their tales sung alongside those of the gods, such as Odin and his hammering son, Thor.

But the Vikings of history have also left behind them some fascinating questions.

How could a people with such blustery prowess on the battlefield also create such an extraordinarily rich culture? Were they horn-helmeted, mead-swilling killers, or a brilliant society of hunters, craftsmen and tradesmen who opened up vast trade routes throughout Europe and Asia, and created empires of barter that helped save the global economy?

In fact, the Vikings were all these things and much more. As explorers, they discovered Iceland, Greenland and North America, and expanded Dublin and areas in and around Russia. As shipbuilders, they perfected willowy vessels that were buoyant in even the shallowest rivers, and others that carried tons of goods across oceans. As leaders and lawgivers, they ruled with a kind of just jurisprudence, including extending myriad rights to women. And as messengers of the word of God, these ex-pagans spread the Gospel with a repent-or-die resolve that remade the world.

And it is that world you'll get to see in the pages of this book. It will take you across the waters and into battle with these fierce fighters. You'll meet the most famous and infamous figures of legend, from Erik the Red and Leif Erikson to Canute the Great and Ragnar Lothbrok. The swiftest ships, the most dazzling riches, the stirring sagas, the art and culture, the truest facts and the unique trade towns are all explored. For the faithful traveler, we cover the best vacation spots to visit today to see

the world on which the Scandinavians left their true marks; for folks who prefer their learning on the couch, we present the 10 greatest film sagas covering the Viking Age.

We need all the aid we can get when it comes to these confounding conquerors who ruled lands and then, in time, simply blended in, to the point where Viking culture is wholly a thing of the past. Their habit of embracing the qualities of culture they saw as superior in England, France, Germany and the rest of the world, from language to currency and politics, served them well at the time, but it ultimately proved to be their undoing.

"The Vikings are capable, it seems, of absorbing what works in a particular place, so they'll ditch their native traditions and accept things around them," says Lars Brownworth, author of *The Sea Wolves: A History of the Vikings*. "And then over about three or four generations, that Viking culture is gone. When you blend in, you disappear."

Not quite. In fact, the Vikings left a legacy richer than any culture of their era. And it's celebrated here, in song and sea battle, in heroes and heroines, in quests and questions, and in a shared legacy that still astounds.

—*Robert Edelstein*

THREE CENTURIES OF RAIDING AND RULING

THE NOTORIOUS NORSEMEN
WEREN'T BORN BATTLE-READY: FROM
SHIPBUILDING TO SWORD-WIELDING,
IT TOOK AN ARMY TO WIN THE WAR.

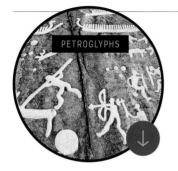
PETROGLYPHS

A LONG

1000 B.C. Before the Vikings were a blip on the radar of history, a Proto-Germanic people begin to settle in what would become the modern countries of Norway, Sweden, Denmark and Finland. Originally farmers and fishermen, they start to develop the culture, language and customs that would eventually become synonymous with the Vikings.

787 A.D. The Vikings start to test their strength, sailing from Norway to the Isle of Portland in the English Channel to attack and pillage the village. This is the first known Viking raid, and therefore, the villagers first assume—quite mistakenly—that their Norse neighbors have arrived in peace.

793 Viking warriors sail to England to ransack a monastery on the island of Lindisfarne, the first raid on English territory. This greatly upsets the locals, who see the raid as a direct attack on Christian society.

794/795 The Norse continue their expansion, invading nearby Scotland and Ireland, including the isles of Skye, Iona and Rathlin. Many communities are forced to relocate farther inland and abandon smaller islands and coastal towns—and to acquiesce to the pagan pillagers.

CHARLEMAGNE

814 The death of Charlemagne is a boon to Viking support: As Austrian professor and Germanist Rudolf Simek wrote, "It is not a coincidence if the early Viking activity occurred during the reign of Charlemagne," as the ruler stoked anti-pagan sentiments.

MONASTERY

DANES LANDING IN ENGLAND

REIGN OF

840 Viking settlers begin spending winters in Ireland, founding the city of Dublin.

844 After a successful raid on Seville in Spain, the Vikings are quickly halted by a Muslim army.

851 Continuing their conquest, the Norse raid Wales for the first time.

860 Rus Vikings (rulers of Finland and Russia who arrived from Sweden) attack Constantinople with 200 shiploads of soldiers.

867 The Vikings murder the king of Northumbria and then capture the city of York, which becomes their English capital.

INVASION OF NORTHUMBRIA

871 Alfred the Great becomes king of Wessex, halting the advance of the Danish Vikings in England.

Under Alfred's watch, Viking leader Guthrum converts to Christianity.

ALFRED THE GREAT

TERROR

The first king of Norway, Harald Fairhair, rules between 872 and 930.

RURIK

HARALD FAIRHAIR

PRINCE OLEG

ROLLO

872 Norwegians flee to Iceland and nearby islands as Harald Fairhair continues to unify Norway. After winning the Battle of Hafrsfjord, he finds himself king of Norway.

879 Viking leader Rurik establishes Kiev, making it the center of the Kievan Rus' domains; he is succeeded by Prince Oleg.

886 Danelaw is established in a treaty between Alfred and Guthrum, legally dividing England.

900 The Norsemen begin raiding along the Mediterranean coast, opening up new trade routes to Arab lands.

911 Charles the Simple, king of France, cedes part of the countryside to the powerful Viking chief Rollo. It is dubbed Normandy (the land of Northmen).

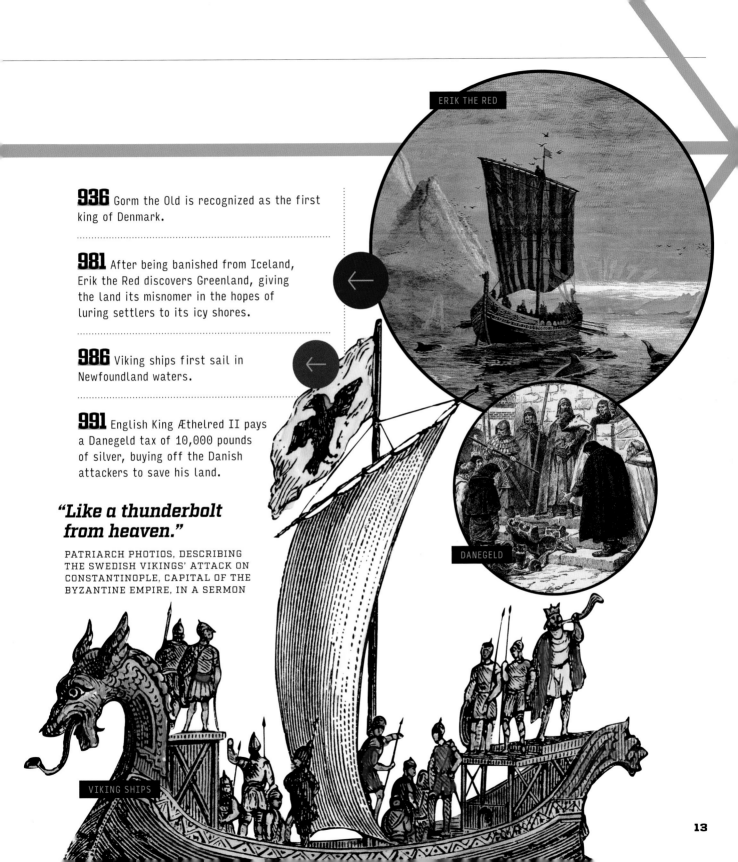

936 Gorm the Old is recognized as the first king of Denmark.

981 After being banished from Iceland, Erik the Red discovers Greenland, giving the land its misnomer in the hopes of luring settlers to its icy shores.

986 Viking ships first sail in Newfoundland waters.

991 English King Æthelred II pays a Danegeld tax of 10,000 pounds of silver, buying off the Danish attackers to save his land.

"Like a thunderbolt from heaven."

PATRIARCH PHOTIOS, DESCRIBING THE SWEDISH VIKINGS' ATTACK ON CONSTANTINOPLE, CAPITAL OF THE BYZANTINE EMPIRE, IN A SERMON

ERIK THE RED

DANEGELD

VIKING SHIPS

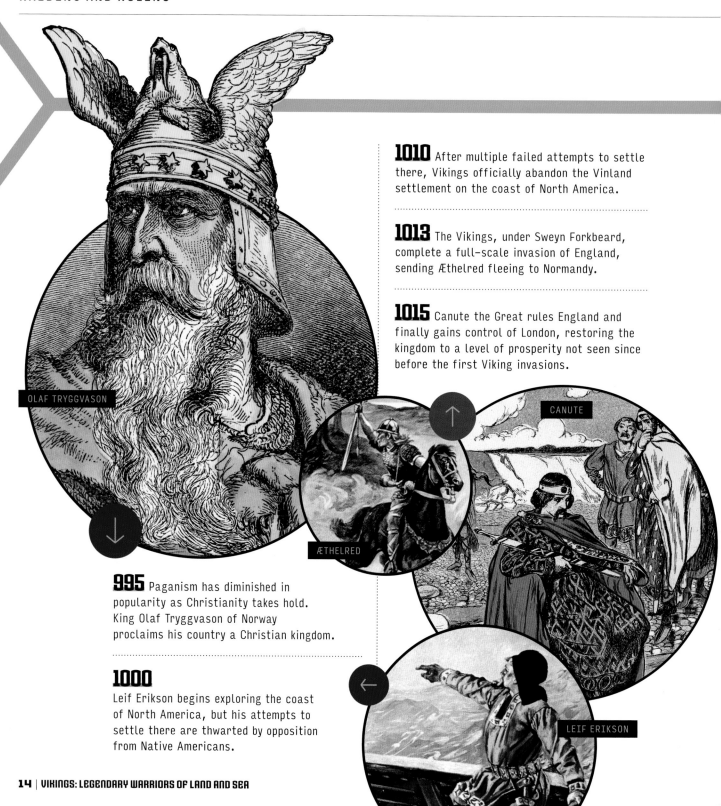

OLAF TRYGGVASON

1010 After multiple failed attempts to settle there, Vikings officially abandon the Vinland settlement on the coast of North America.

1013 The Vikings, under Sweyn Forkbeard, complete a full-scale invasion of England, sending Æthelred fleeing to Normandy.

1015 Canute the Great rules England and finally gains control of London, restoring the kingdom to a level of prosperity not seen since before the first Viking invasions.

CANUTE

ÆTHELRED

995 Paganism has diminished in popularity as Christianity takes hold. King Olaf Tryggvason of Norway proclaims his country a Christian kingdom.

1000

Leif Erikson begins exploring the coast of North America, but his attempts to settle there are thwarted by opposition from Native Americans.

LEIF ERIKSON

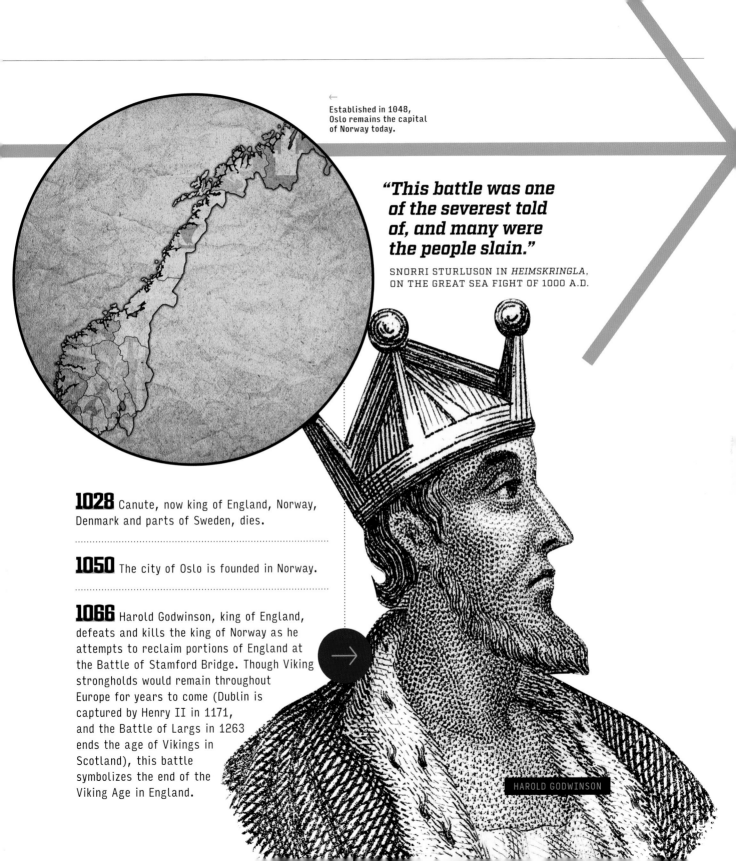

←
Established in 1048,
Oslo remains the capital
of Norway today.

*"This battle was one
of the severest told
of, and many were
the people slain."*

SNORRI STURLUSON IN *HEIMSKRINGLA*,
ON THE GREAT SEA FIGHT OF 1000 A.D.

1028 Canute, now king of England, Norway,
Denmark and parts of Sweden, dies.

1050 The city of Oslo is founded in Norway.

1066 Harold Godwinson, king of England,
defeats and kills the king of Norway as he
attempts to reclaim portions of England at
the Battle of Stamford Bridge. Though Viking
strongholds would remain throughout
Europe for years to come (Dublin is
captured by Henry II in 1171,
and the Battle of Largs in 1263
ends the age of Vikings in
Scotland), this battle
symbolizes the end of the
Viking Age in England.

HAROLD GODWINSON

THE PLUNDER BEGINS

IT TURNS OUT THE VIKINGS HAD A WORLD OF REASONS FOR STARTING THEIR VANQUISHING CONQUESTS.

T hey were "vile people," according to the old texts, who came out of nowhere like a terrorizing whirlwind along the seas. Savages, they were, these bearded, pagan Norsemen in their longships. Oh, if only the monks of Northumbria—the kingdom that, in 793, connected Northern England with Southern Scotland—had heeded the "foreboding omens" history would one day record, describing the sacking that started the Viking Age.

As the words set down in the *Anglo-Saxon Chronicle* years later recalled, these omens

→
If the monks thought God would protect them, they were sadly mistaken at Lindisfarne in 793.

"wretchedly terrified the people. There were... lightning storms; and fiery dragons were seen flying in the sky." These signs were followed by great famine, and shortly after in the same year, on June 8, "the ravaging of heathen men destroyed God's church at Lindisfarne through brutal robbery and slaughter."

Of course, that's how the English saw it. Those pagan Vikings? They were too busy robbing the famed church at Lindisfarne to put any iron gall ink to parchment.

Still, historians generally acknowledge that the timeline for Viking exploits—the 300 years of raids and conquests; trading expeditions and land explorations; and ruled countries and religious conversions that rerouted the course of world history—began in 793 on that rocky Northumbrian shore. The Lindisfarne monks were either killed or disbursed, and much booty was taken and brought back to Scandinavia. But those same historians grapple with—and, frankly, have long argued about—what came before the raid. Why did the Norsemen set off to plunder in the first place?

"That right there is the great Viking question," says Lars Brownworth, author of *The Sea Wolves: A History of the Vikings*, among several books about the period. "Why did it all start?"

Speculation about several reasons persist to this day, and they all seem to smack of varying degrees of plausibility.

It Was About Demographics

An increase in the population? An ancient instance of climate change? The need for more land to work? For historians, these three ideas seem to swirl together to create one possible motive for the move outward toward other civilizations. True, Norway and Denmark were not immune to the worldwide baby boom of the era, and it's hard to accurately settle on a perfect evidential start for the Medieval Warm Period, which made the icy waters much easier to traverse. Plus, the boom may well have caused competition for the most tillable land.

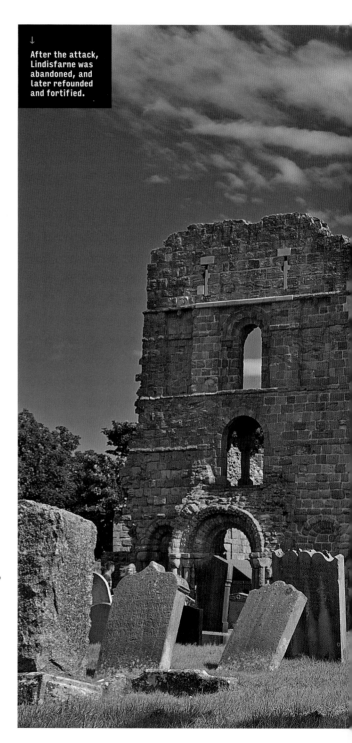

↓ After the attack, Lindisfarne was abandoned, and later refounded and fortified.

ODIN

ANGLO-SAXON CHRONICLE

And yet, these notions offer a perspective that doesn't necessarily apply quite so specifically to the Norse and the Danes. Most estimates put the Warm Period at a somewhat later date, which would have affected the likes of Leif Erikson, who made his way around to the New World some 200 years later. According to James H. Barrett, a professor of archaeology and anthropology at the U.K.'s University of Cambridge, the evidence more suggests the population moved around within the confines of Scandinavia as opposed to outside it.

It Was About Marriage

A more pressing issue in terms of the people involved the imbalance between the sexes. You may have a population explosion, but what if the shocking occurrence of female infanticide goes along with it? Enough indications exist that boys were preferable to girls among births...leading to the idea that some newborn girls may have been killed in Scandinavian society.

If that was the case, the disparity would have come back to haunt everybody as generations came of age. A higher population of men ultimately led to a more militaristic society, brotherhoods of brethren beating their chests and doing battle among themselves and neighboring areas. But a little time passed and suddenly the lower number of women led to a higher demand for wives. And demand, in this case, equaled dowry. Plunder could provide the cash needed to accrue the "bride-price" necessary to win a woman and buy a home, according to Barrett.

It Was About Politics

Bride-price wasn't the only factor involved. Trade routes had opened up, bringing in more valuable metals and creating the Iron Age in Scandinavia, leading to a shift in societies from tribes to smaller kingdoms. And with everybody fighting for their own piece of pride and power, too many young men found themselves shut out.

The seas, however, and the lands beyond proved to be the great equalizer. England, France, Germany and Russia had their own politics—and observations based on years of trading partnerships showed that the coffers of the kings of Europe were bulging. Those leaders were often old and lazy, or, at the very least, unprepared for conquest.

"The Vikings had these kind of mass migrations before and they're coming into contact with the Roman world," says Brownworth. "Even their language is based on Etruscan scripts [from Italy]. So there was definitely contact there, and it seems the bulk of this came from trade, so this is how they are made aware of what's going on around them."

That awareness led to strategy and action— something the European leaders never counted on—with the lure of riches too great to ignore.

> ## "From the time the Vikings came to the attention of the annalists of England, the view was they were engaged in a religious war."
>
> HISTORIAN ROBERT FERGUSON

"As long as you have a little bit of daring and luck, anything is possible," says Brownworth. "The Vikings come crashing into these kind of controlled states and decaying worlds and you know, there are so many of them. Take [Norman adventurer] Robert Guiscard, who starts life as the sixth son of his family: He has zero prospects. And he ends up defeating the Byzantine emperor, and losing one battle his entire career; he's the master of all southern Italy and aiming for a good deal more. That's a stunning possibility, and it's exciting."

It Was About the Gods

That one-eyed, long-bearded, spear-carrying, cloak-wearing, broad-hatted man of mythology named Odin ruled the pagan roost among the Norse gods when the Viking era began. Granted, there's no small irony in the fact that so much of Viking culture would eventually embrace the tenets of Christ. But no great allegiance existed when longships first sailed down toward Europe.

And that made the sacking of Lindisfarne all the more egregious. For England, the robbing of a monastery and the violent killings of the monks who lived there served not only as an affront, but as a crime against Christ. For the Vikings, however, it simply meant access to the most valuable goods available, since, as they discovered again and again in the first several years of their raids, the churches were well stocked. Oh, for Odin's sake, things got out of hand!

It Was About Adventure

Young men sailing together toward a future full of bounty. A camaraderie of purpose in plunder. And to this you can add "silver fever."

In terms of available and desirable bounty, silver was, relatively speaking, a newer deal. The shiny stuff had just begun to flood into Scandinavia through trade. Its worth was obvious; its availability in Europe seemed prevalent. And it sure helped in bride-price.

It Was About New Maritime Design

All these factors were a call to action for the men of Denmark, Norway and other points north to venture out with a head of steam to lands in the south and begin robbing, pillaging, raiding, burning, conquering and—in a word—winning. But the means to do all of this wasn't truly available to them until their longships became products of more astonishing and innovative designs. And for Brownworth, that really began with one important foundational change to the way the ships were made.

"It's the development of the keel, which makes transatlantic voyages possible," he says.

If longships had been around since perhaps 400 B.C., it wasn't until the year 700 that the first true keel ship was constructed. The several-section wooden keel, designed as an inverted "T" shape, allowed for line after line of overlapping planks that were joined upon it from stem to stern. A thin depth made the ships extraordinarily swift, with an ability to carry great weights, while also being sure enough at sea to withstand even the rockiest of weather conditions. In a sense, no ambitions among the Vikings ultimately could have been realized without the creation of the keel.

"It made transatlantic voyages possible with lethal speed and an ability to go up rivers that are relatively shallow," says Brownworth. "As a side note—and I find this terrifying—[it made it so] you were up on deck, maybe with a tent, crossing the Atlantic in whatever weather, and there was about an inch of oakwood between you and the ocean. But it's the keel as a technological ability, put together with all the wealth and the weakness of [European] empires that, I think, is what initially drew them."

After being drawn in, there would be little stopping the Vikings from continuing their pursuits, which redistributed wealth and power throughout the European kingdom for more than 300 years, beginning with that fateful June day in Northumbria.

"You have the first taste with that attack on Lindisfarne where you're coming back loaded to the gills with wealth. And to the Vikings, it really must've seemed like winning the lottery," says Brownworth. "You know, here's an area, which is totally cut off from the rest of the land, totally run over from the sea, with lots of wealth guarded by old men. To the Vikings, that must have been, 'Perfect: Yes, please.'"

LEGEND HAS IT

How terrifying were the Vikings? An 11 on a scale of 1–10, according to Alcuin, a local scholar at the time of the Lindisfarne attack. "The heathens poured out the blood of saints around the altar and trampled on the bodies of saints in the temple of God, like dung in the streets... behold the church spattered with the blood of the priests of God," he wrote. The word of their savagery became the normal perception of the Vikings for centuries thereafter, until tales of their conversion and assimilation—and the violence of opposing rulers such as Charlemagne—became better known.

→ A 12th-century
illuminated manuscript
shows the Vikings
surrounding the church.

THE MASTERS

The Berserkers of old got themselves into trances before heading into fierce battle.

The beastly cry of the pagans that landed like a spear-point of fear in the hearts of lesser men of battle. The terrible, and terribly deserved, reputation for violence that preceded their every move. The knowledge that they were gluttons for glory in every fight. It's true: You messed with the Vikings at your own peril.

Modern scholarship, as it often does, has made great strides at retooling the view of these men and women of valor. They were poets and politicians, thinkers and tinkerers, and if they conquered they also compromised.

The new saga translations, however, do not skimp on the military might that brought the Vikings this notorious fame in the first place. Yes, there are now emotional backstories and tales of love and wonder. But there are also, as one story suggests, still the drunken preschoolers chopping people in half.

OF

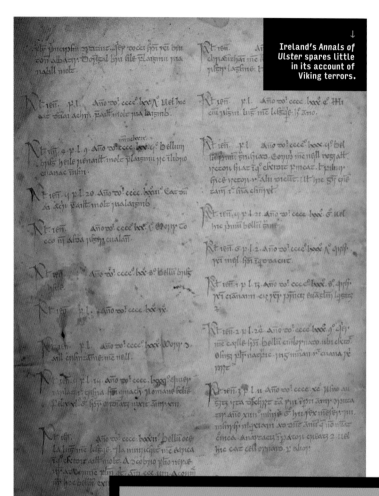

↓
Ireland's Annals of Ulster spares little in its account of Viking terrors.

"They're ultraviolent, and I was thinking, what is so attractive about the Vikings for the modern world?" wonders Lars Brownworth, author of *The Sea Wolves: A History of the Vikings*, among other books about the period. "And I was listening to a political speech and it struck me that we live in a very focus-grouped world where everything is so carefully considered. And I think it's kind of refreshing to read about the Vikings, where what you see is what you get. They are unscripted and they're out to grab as much as they can."

That said, Brownworth acknowledges the route to victory wasn't at all impulsive; their incredible mastery of the art of war propelled them from being heathen outsiders to rulers of European lands in a matter of only decades. "They're portrayed as these brutes," he says, "and yet they're extremely knowledgeable." Their unparalleled success can best be summed up by these 10 principles of plunder.

1 They Knew How to Navigate

The supposition of Viking knowledge of the tides, cloud formations, bird flight patterns, landmarks and what historian Robert Ferguson has called "a developed sensitivity to the subtleties of sea, sky and weather in excess of anything we possess now"

LEGEND HAS IT

The *berserkir* notion has a special place in the sagas, perhaps because the literature seems exaggerated beyond all bounds. As Anders Winroth writes in *The Age of the Vikings*, one warrior named Harthben used his hours of pre-fighting bloodlust to some acclaim. "A demonical frenzy suddenly possessed him, he furiously bit and devoured the rim of his shield; he gulped down fiery coals without a qualm and let them pass down into his belly; he ran the gauntlet of crackling flames; and finally when he had raved through every sort of madness, he turned his sword with raging hand against the hearts of six of his henchmen [who had been known to conspire against him]." Oh yes, and only *then* did he venture into battle! No small wonder his opponents were shaking in their boots.

only tells part of the story. The Norsemen and Danes also had something of a sixth sense about locations for fights, along with ideas about timing that confounded attack victims. "They know when Easter is so they can attack then; they know where the centers are and where there's wealth," says Brownworth. "They're extremely canny."

2 They Knew When to Go Berserk

In a sense, the Vikings were somewhat like today's terrorists. You fought bravely, and even if you died, your reward was a lifetime of feasting in the glory place of Valhalla. As to the fight itself, for the most focused of warriors, it was preceded by hours of what was known as "berserkir" behavior, which amounted to whipping oneself into a frenzy that became a great inspiration once the battle began. The term is the basis for the modern word "berserk" for good reason, and has lent a certain inspiration to professional athletes getting themselves in the right mindset before a big game.

3 They Followed the Hird

That *hird* was their word for the professional soldiers each of the kings and battle leaders surrounded themselves with. These soldiers were highly trained, loyal killing machines, and they were usually the ones called upon in smaller raids. For larger battles, a kind of draft system called the *leidang* was put in place so local farmers could be trained to fight. Communities were also commissioned to build as many longships as were needed for plundering or protecting. It wasn't smart to avoid the draft in this case; doing so led to fines or violence.

4 They Knew What They Wanted

So much of the early literature about Viking raids had to do with the terrible insult to Christ delivered by the church-plundering heathens. If only that were the true goal in the first place. For the Vikings, it wasn't that the churches were the centers of God; it's that they were the centers of goods. The golden crucifixes and gem-encrusted gospel pieces were much more valuable when it came to trade, financial standing and the money needed to either secure a bride through dowry or a house back home.

That said…

5 They Were Facing Weakened Opponents

Part of that weakness was psychological and began with those church raids. The Old Testament's Book of Jeremiah had foretold of "an army coming from the north…armed with bows and spears; they are cruel and without mercy…. They come like men in battle formation to attack you, Daughter Babylon." Monks had decried Europe's lack of piety as the

> ## "Starting in 845, the Danegeld payment became a money-with-menaces tactic the Vikings would employ with great success in England."
>
> HISTORIAN ROBERT FERGUSON

reason for the raids. And once the churches—and then the kingdoms in England, Ireland, France and Germany—began to experience the wrath of the warriors, they too felt overwhelmed.

6 They Were Strategically Sound

The Vikings relied on the element of surprise, which made it easier to attack defenseless, landlocked countries that were rich in resources and women. As was written in medieval Ireland's *Annals of Ulster*, "The sea spewed forth floods of foreigners into Erin, so that no haven, no landing-place, no stronghold, no fort, no castle might be found, but it was submerged by waves of Vikings and pirates." It was nearly impossible to defend against grand lines of troops coming in from the seas—or from footholds they'd established—without any warning. "It's not like they're such fantastic fighters; they're *predators*," says Brownworth. "And they know when to strike."

7 They Fought Well on Both Land and Sea

The raids led to further inroads in Europe, with battle leaders forming huge standing armies, each with troops who knew that, beyond group glory, individual achievement would be recognized and rewarded. But it was at sea that the Vikings showed their true colors as fighters—although, strangely enough, it was always about in-fighting. "For almost 250 years, there was not a significant naval battle in the North Atlantic that wasn't Viking against Viking," says Brownworth.

8 They Had a Feel for Fighting Tactics

It was one thing to take advantage of the *berserkir* idea; that always helped once the battle cry was sounded. It was also the swine array, as historian Angus Konstam writes, that worked against the Anglo-Saxon standing army. In the array, "warriors adopted a wedge-shaped arrow formation to attack an enemy shieldwall, behind which archers aim defensive volleys," Konstam writes in *Historical Atlas of the Viking World*. In that shieldwall—or *skjaldborgr* in the old scripts—shields were overlapped much the way planks of wood attached to keels on longships overlapped, creating a protective barrier that ran through horizontal lines of fighters.

↓ Saxon hammered silver coins from the early 11th century lined Viking pockets.

↓ Silver booty was a popular choice for Danegeld, which enriched the Viking warriors.

9 They Sported Weapons That Suited Their Purpose

Racing toward the enemy, wearing tunics and chain mail, carrying metal-reinforced wooden shields, the Viking warriors had spears and sometimes swords that were tactically made for quick and easy killing. Their light and strong, groove-bladed, double-edged long swords had blunt points, meaning they were used more for slashing motions than stabbing ones. (Swords made by Ulfberht, fashioned from the finest steel brought in from Asia, were considered the best.)

Stabbing came courtesy of the straight-bladed spears, featuring broad blades with well-placed cross guards that prevented the spears from penetrating too deeply. That made their removal from a victim's body much less problematic—an important advantage when battles continued. Danes preferred two-handed axes for cleaving through thick armor or even a helmet; smaller

"The name of King Magnus's [king of Norway and Denmark] ax, 'Hel,' is also the name of the Norse goddess of death. This hellishly efficient weapon is the very ax still portrayed in the Norwegian national coat of arms."

HISTORIAN ANDERS WINROTH

axes were for tossing, and bows and arrows also came in handy. And those helmets with signature nose flanges continue to bring Vikings renown. As to those horned helmets? They were *never* worn in battle, regardless of their rep.

10 They Knew How to Exact a Worthy Bribe

Starting in the 850s, it was recorded that Dane Vikings began demanding "tributes" from frightened opponents—sometimes after some of the damage had been done, and sometimes before, just as a warning. This Danegeld was paid so that the Vikings would head off and raid elsewhere. The practice became, in essence, a preferred extortion racket, with the ultimatum extended to anyone who wished to see themselves protected instead of plundered. And the phrase "paying through the nose?" As Konstam points out, that came from Vikings slitting the noses of taxpayers who refused to show them the money.

It was just another proverbial arrow in their military arsenal, keeping opponents at bay for the better part of three centuries. "They have this strategy and tactic of battle unforeseen prior to their appearance," says Brownworth. "Not only are their offensives keeping everyone off guard, their defenses and fortifications (see sidebar, right) are also pretty impregnable. When it comes to war, they're a complete culture."

↑
A plate found in Sweden shows Odin, alongside a Berserker with battling in mind.

HOLDING DOWN THE FORT

When necessary, Danish kings built defenses every bit as impressive as their offensive means.

Were they boot camps built by warriors such as Sweyn Forkbeard to train troops, or fortifications meant to protect the likes of Danish King Harald Bluetooth? Not enough is known about the trelleborgs—aka, the Viking ring forts—beyond their geometry and beauty.

Seven such forts have been discovered by archaeologists. Those thought to have been built by Harald are constructed from the same template, beginning with a giant 500-foot perfect circle that looks like something out of an M. Night Shyamalan movie, with outer and inner walls that had four entryways to correspond with compass points. The interior was divided by wood streets into quarters; each was filled by buildings of varying number and size for living, working and storage.

Internal courtyards were perhaps used for drilling the troops. The trelleborgs were each on a steep bank with a moat located outside the grounds.

The structures made for unique defenses, but perhaps more than anything, they stand as symbols of royal power in Denmark. The largest, Aggersborg, has an inner diameter of nearly 800 feet. Even now, they stand out from the Danish countryside as unique relics of a storied age.

↓
The circular structures were designed with defensive measures in mind.

TRAPPINGS OF BATTLE

THE WEAPONS AND WARDROBES USED BY VIKING WARRIORS.

A military force couldn't enjoy the widespread success the Vikings achieved at the end of the first millennium without a well-executed plan. For the Norsemen, this included an abundance of some of the finest armor and weaponry of their era. Harnessing the talents of blacksmiths, woodcarvers and other craftsmen, the Vikings could wield weapons with the best of them. Life for freemen was more precarious than that of the higher class: A farmer likely owned just a spear and shield, while intricate armor was built and available for the extremely wealthy, nobility and professional warriors.

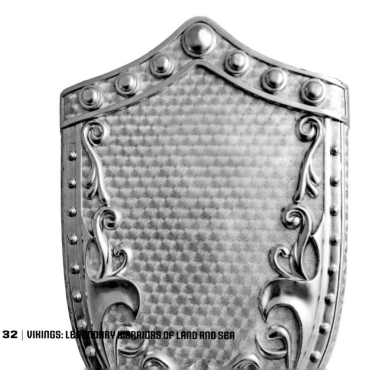

←

While shield shapes varied, kite shields like this are thought to have been brought to Europe by the Vikings.

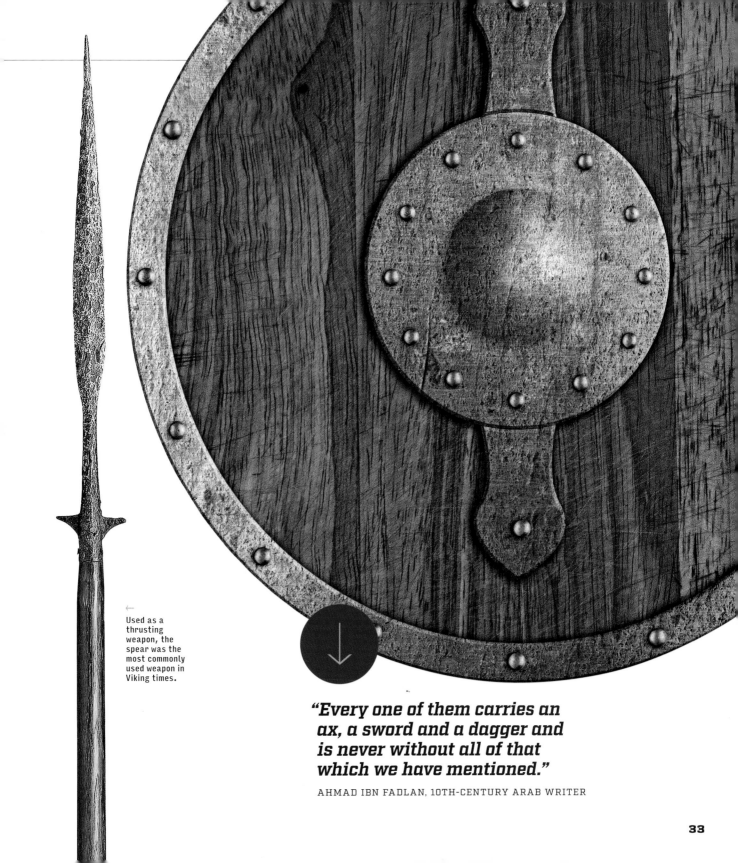

Used as a thrusting weapon, the spear was the most commonly used weapon in Viking times.

"Every one of them carries an ax, a sword and a dagger and is never without all of that which we have mentioned."

AHMAD IBN FADLAN, 10TH-CENTURY ARAB WRITER

→ Horned helmets were a construct of 19th-century Romanticism.

← Without standard armor, Vikings made do with what they had. In one historic saga, a fighter protected himself with flat stones beneath his clothing.

On the Offense

Few things distinguished a Viking like his sword. A mark of prestige and power, the craftsmanship was advanced, making it rare and often the most valuable item a Viking man would ever own. While the majority of weapons used by the maritime warriors were spears and axes, the most common sword was undoubtedly a double-edged iron model, measuring about 3 feet in length. The most expensive and impressive was the single-handed variety, its longer shape making it easier to hold a shield at the same time. In the *Laxdaela Saga*, a sword was said to be worth a half ark of gold,

"It's quite unusual to find remnants from the Viking Age that are so well-preserved.... It might be used today if you sharpened the edge."

COUNTY CONSERVATOR PER MORTEN EKERHOVD, ON THE 2015 DISCOVERY OF A VIKING SWORD IN NORWAY

→
A leather pouch with brass
trim might hold coins,
weapons or even pendants.

or 16 milk cows, a large sum of money for the time, and a status symbol above all other.

For those who could not afford or were not lucky enough to inherit a sword, the weapons of choice for many warriors was an ax, a bow and arrow, or a spear. These items were often found in the burial grounds of middle-class men who would go off and fight, then come home and tend to the family farm. While nearly all men in Viking society owned some sort of weapon, without the money or the clout,

their options were severely limited to less-effective means of battle.

A Viking in Shining Armor

No, Norsemen's helmets didn't *actually* have horns—despite the enduring stereotype that has followed the Vikings for over 1,000 years. Helmet designs in the era were actually very simple: a few pieces of iron riveted together into a bowl shape. This technique required less effort than the style

→
Because Vikings
were largely
farmers, the ax
was an everyday
item each man was
expected to own.

←
Tales tell of
weapons so
powerful they
could break a
foe's sword
in two.

→
In 1943, the first
Viking helmet
was discovered in
Norway; it's the
only one found
that could be
reconstructed.

popular before and after the Viking Age, which required just one large piece of iron hammered into shape.

In battle, helmets were likely marked to distinguish between opposing forces, and despite the protection helmets provided, warriors knew that a sword wielded just the right way could slice through their headgear. In *Egil's Saga*, there's the tale of a warrior who, in a wild frenzy, swings his weapon at the head of a Viking fighter so hard it splits clear through his helmet and skull, picking the entire man up in the air on the edge of the ax.

Taking a look at the laws of the time, it's clear safety was a priority, but there was little that could be regulated without a means to assign each man a set of armor. In Gulating, one of the first Norwegian legislative assemblies, it was written that every man on a leading ship was required by law to have a shield on board. The first—and sometimes only—level of defense, shields were

> "Archaeologists find [weapons] in graves, lakes, near fords and at battlefields from the Viking period. Each find is a small piece in the large jigsaw puzzle of Viking warfare."
>
> NATIONAL MUSEUM OF DENMARK

often brightly colored to distinguish fighters and sometimes to send messages (red and white signifying peace, for instance). It's hard to say for sure what shields were made out of. Those found on the surviving *Gokstad* ship were black and yellow, made of a single layer of planks butted together, but literary sources reveal that shields could also be made of laminated wood. It's likely Vikings were seeking two traits: durable and unlikely to splinter, yet still light to hold and easy to maneuver.

Lower-class men were thought to dress in layers of their thickest fabrics (leather and thick winter wool could both offer limited protection), forming a tenuous barrier between weapon and skin. Some wealthy Vikings adorned themselves in mail shirts, interlinked iron rings riveted together to create a wall between clothing and the weapons that sought to stab. While this may have stopped a knife from cutting too deep, it offered little in the way of protection against the edge of a sword or spear.

A High Price

In the end, even the wealthiest Viking's weaponry and armor wasn't enough to truly protect him against the forces of combat. Large death tolls were common in the all-out bloodbaths that grew synonymous with the Viking name. In the Battle of Stamford Bridge that happened near the end of the era, it's thought that at least 11,000 men died in battle. The loss of life was a high price to pay, but for a people drawn to conquest, and to the promise of the unknown, this was worth the fight. In today's world, these warriors' legacies live on.

10 VIKING BATTLES THAT CHANGED THE WORLD

DISCOVER STORIES OF EUROPEAN RULERS DUELING TO THE DEATH FOR THE PROMISE OF POWER, LAND AND THE CHANCE TO ALTER HISTORY.

↓
"The endless stream of Vikings never ceases to increase," the monk Ermantarius wrote in the ninth century.

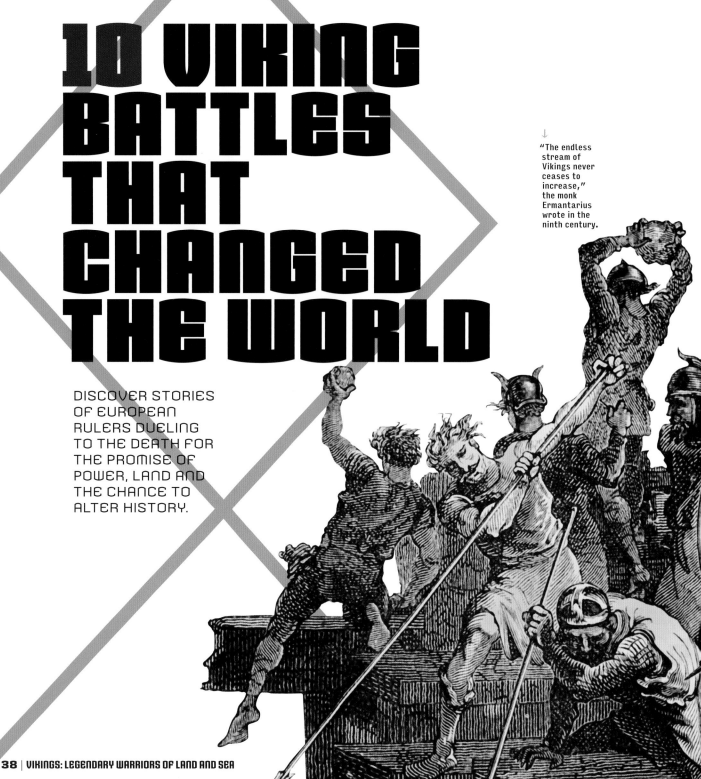

10

Siege of Paris (845)

While most game-changing battles took place in England, Scandinavia and Ireland, the Vikings refused to let Paris out of their sights. In 845, the Vikings' Franco invasion culminated with the Siege of Paris—led by the Norse chieftain Ragnar Lothbrok. Ragnar and his fleet of 120 ships sailed up the river Seine in March 845 to fight Frankish King Charles the Bald and his (considerably smaller) army. By Easter, the Vikings had reached Paris with relative ease, retreating only after plundering and receiving a ransom worth 7,000 *livres* of silver and gold.

→
Olaf traveled with 3,600 men through Sweden to the Battle of Stiklestad.

Battle of Stiklestad

This battle was a good-news/bad-news event for Norway. In the summer of 1030, its Christian Viking King Olaf Haraldsson was defeated and killed fighting in it. The circumstances surrounding his death are questionable, but led to his canonization as the patron saint of Norway and also paved the way for Christianity in Scandinavia and greater Northern Europe in general.

The battle and saint are so lauded, they're still celebrated in Norway today: On Olsog, or St. Olaf's Day, the St. Olav Drama is performed annually, depicting the battle and its aftermath.

9

→ On the third day of battle, Eric listened to Odin, and arrows fell over the Jomsvikings.

8

Battle of Fýrisvellir

In the 980s, tensions were heating up between King Eric the Victorious and his nephew Styrbjörn the Strong as the two fought for the throne of Sweden in the Battle of Fýrisvellir. In a Shakespearean plotline, Styrbjörn, ruler of the Jomsvikings, was determined to lay claim to the crown after being denied it upon his father's death. Suspecting his uncle (King Eric) of poisoning his father, Styrbjörn launched a fiery battle, vowing to never leave Sweden again: His options were simply win or die. Setting his own ships on fire to encourage his men to fight after reaching a Swedish-led impasse, then advancing with the threat of a forest fire at his fingertips, Styrbjörn marched with his Jomsvikings through the countryside. On the third day of the attack, Styrbjörn insisted his men continue to fight— even after all hope of a victory was lost—rushing into the pack of the enemy, where they met with death and defeat.

→ The Battle of Assandun is mentioned in the Knýtlinga Saga.

7

Battle of Assandun

Led by Canute the Great, the Danes declared victory over King Edmund Ironside's English armies on October 18, 1016. The battle was significant, as it marked the conclusion of the Danish reconquest of England. A treaty, signed by Edmund, declared that all of England (except Wessex) would be controlled by Canute.

Battle of Clontarf

In 11th-century Ireland, near a then-tiny village called Dublin, the Battle of Clontarf raged in April 1014. Combat began at sunrise and lasted until the last rays set behind the horizon, killing at least 7,000 men from both the Viking and Leinster forces. The High King of Ireland Brian Boru had his hands full as his troops fought off a Norse-Irish alliance and an external Viking group. The Irish king would come out victorious, but regrettably, not alive. King Brian, his son Murchad and his grandson Toirdelbach would all perish in the battle—alongside nearly everyone fighting. It's believed just 100 of the king's men and 20 Dublinmen survived. After an especially long and bloody battle, things truly went awry when, after the Vikings withdrew toward their ships, the tide came in, carrying the boats away and in turn drowning many of the surviving warriors.

→
Like Hitler or Elvis, King Olaf "sightings" continued for decades after the battle.

←
High King of Ireland Brian Boru reigned for 12 years before his demise at the Battle of Clontarf.

Battle of Svolder

As the Danish continued to seek control of Norway in the late 900s, trouble was brewing in the western Baltic Sea. With much at stake—like the reunification of Norway and the spread of Christianity in Scandinavia—Norway's King Olaf Tryggvason was ambushed by an alliance of enemies, including the kings of Denmark and Sweden, as well as Eric Hákonarson, Jarl of Lade, while sailing home from Pomerania. Olaf was woefully overmatched, battling 70 warships with his fleet of 11. After each boat was captured, Olaf allegedly threw himself overboard into the sea, unable to witness his foes' final victory, and the Jarls of Lade ruled Norway as a fief of Denmark and Sweden.

While most sources report Olaf's apparent suicide, there are conflicting sagas, some suggesting the ousted king made his way to land through a variety of good fortune—from swimming through friendly waters, to angels, to a Wendish ship rescue.

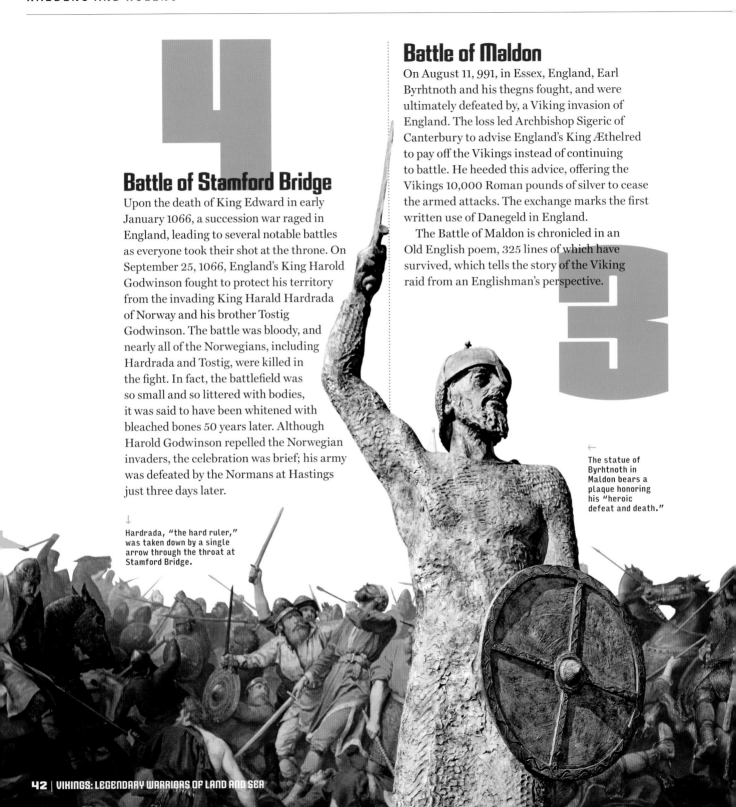

4

Battle of Stamford Bridge

Upon the death of King Edward in early January 1066, a succession war raged in England, leading to several notable battles as everyone took their shot at the throne. On September 25, 1066, England's King Harold Godwinson fought to protect his territory from the invading King Harald Hardrada of Norway and his brother Tostig Godwinson. The battle was bloody, and nearly all of the Norwegians, including Hardrada and Tostig, were killed in the fight. In fact, the battlefield was so small and so littered with bodies, it was said to have been whitened with bleached bones 50 years later. Although Harold Godwinson repelled the Norwegian invaders, the celebration was brief; his army was defeated by the Normans at Hastings just three days later.

↓
Hardrada, "the hard ruler," was taken down by a single arrow through the throat at Stamford Bridge.

Battle of Maldon

On August 11, 991, in Essex, England, Earl Byrhtnoth and his thegns fought, and were ultimately defeated by, a Viking invasion of England. The loss led Archbishop Sigeric of Canterbury to advise England's King Æthelred to pay off the Vikings instead of continuing to battle. He heeded this advice, offering the Vikings 10,000 Roman pounds of silver to cease the armed attacks. The exchange marks the first written use of Danegeld in England.

The Battle of Maldon is chronicled in an Old English poem, 325 lines of which have survived, which tells the story of the Viking raid from an Englishman's perspective.

3

←
The statue of Byrhtnoth in Maldon bears a plaque honoring his "heroic defeat and death."

→ Guthrum, defeated by Alfred, later converted to Christianity.

Battle of Edington

For years, beginning in the late 700s, Viking raids involved limited bloodshed as England's northern neighbors arrived on their coast to raid and settle. That all changed with the arrival of the Danish "Great Army" in 865. The Great Army's goal was, plain and simple, to conquer. By 878, the Danish army held East and Northeast England, and were headed for Wessex, leading to the Battle of Edington. Between May 6 and May 12, 878, the Great Heathen Army faced off against Alfred the Great and the defenders of his Wessex kingdom. Alfred fought "ferociously, forming a dense shieldwall against the whole army of the pagans, and striving long and bravely...overthrew the pagans with great slaughter," according to the ecclesiastical chronicler of *The Medieval Life of King Alfred the Great*. The victory was so critical to England, it is said to have saved Anglo-Saxon independence.

"[King Alfred] overthrew the pagans with great slaughter."

FROM *THE MEDIEVAL LIFE OF KING ALFRED THE GREAT*

Battle of Hastings

The high of his win at the Battle of Stamford Bridge was exceedingly short for Harold Godwinson, who had been fending off attacks on all sides for years. After Stamford Bridge and the deaths of Tostig and Hardrada, Harold had almost rid himself of serious enemies—with just William, Duke of Normandy, left to contend with.

William and his forces invaded just three days after the Battle of Stamford Bridge, catching Harold and his still-recovering forces off guard. Harold headed south, gathering around 7,000 forces as he marched, but the victory was a decisive Norman one. The battle roared on from dawn till dusk on October 14, 1066, and it wasn't until Harold's death that his men retreated. William was crowned king on December 25, 1066. Alongside the Stamford Bridge, this is customarily called the end of the Viking Age.

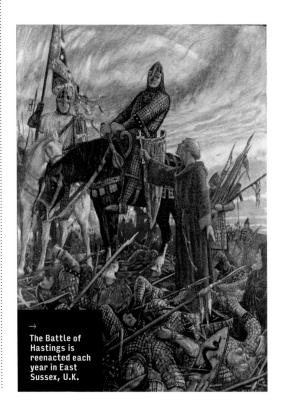

→ The Battle of Hastings is reenacted each year in East Sussex, U.K.

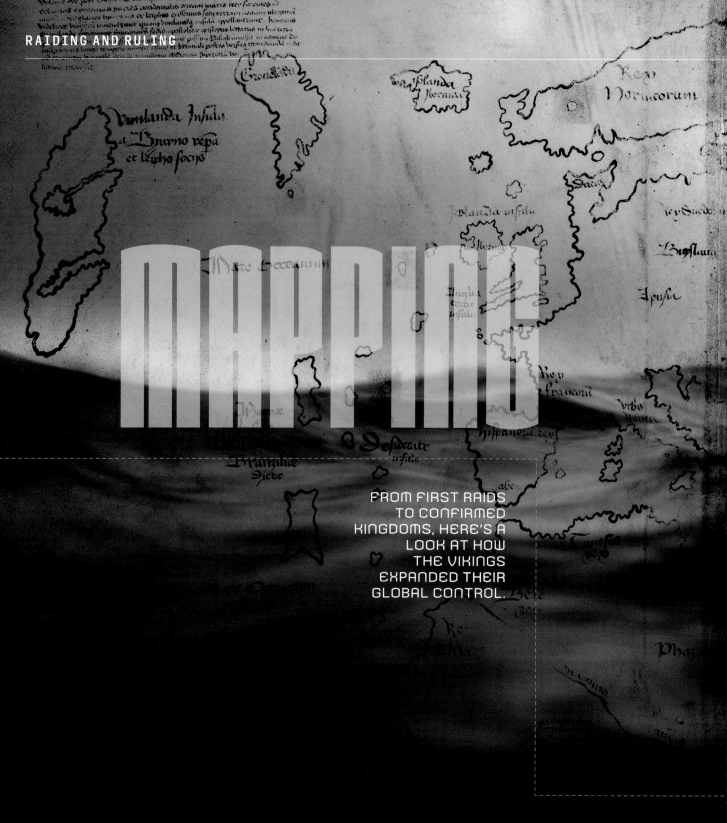

MAPPING

FROM FIRST RAIDS
TO CONFIRMED
KINGDOMS, HERE'S A
LOOK AT HOW
THE VIKINGS
EXPANDED THEIR
GLOBAL CONTROL.

THEIR WORLD

ONCE THE VIKINGS TASTED THE SUCCESS OF CONQUEST, THERE WAS LITTLE REASON TO SQUANDER WHAT THEY SAW AS A WORLD-DOMINATING OPPORTUNITY.

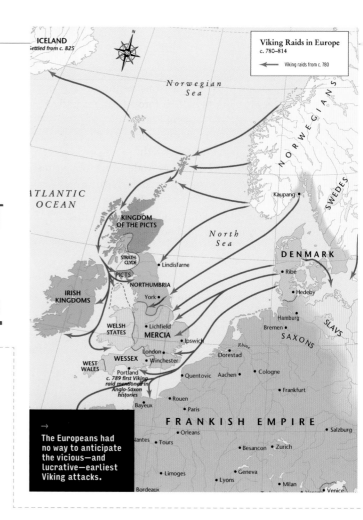

Viking Raids in Europe
c. 780–814

⟵ Viking raids from c. 780

ICELAND
Settled from c. 825

Norwegian Sea

NORWEGIANS

SWEDES

ATLANTIC OCEAN

North Sea

Kaupang

KINGDOM OF THE PICTS

STRATH CLYDE

PICTS

NORTHUMBRIA

Lindisfarne

York

IRISH KINGDOMS

DENMARK

Ribe

Hedeby

WELSH STATES

Lichfield

MERCIA

Ipswich

Hamburg

Bremen

SAXONS

SLAVS

Rhine

London

Winchester

Dorestad

Cologne

WEST WALES

WESSEX

Portland
c. 789 first Viking raid mentioned in Anglo-Saxon histories

Quentovic

Aachen

Frankfurt

Rouen

Paris

Bayeux

FRANKISH EMPIRE

Nantes

Orleans

Salzburg

Tours

Besancon

Zurich

Limoges

Geneva

Lyons

Milan

Venice

Bordeaux

→ The Europeans had no way to anticipate the vicious—and lucrative—earliest Viking attacks.

uropean kingdoms were historically flush and felt utterly invincible—a perception that went tragically wrong for them. For the hungry Norsemen it was, as historian Lars Brownworth put it, "like winning the lottery."

From 793's raid on Lindisfarne, to the Norman Conquest in 1066, the Viking nations won battles and ruled. They roamed the seas and seized inland empires; made chunks of Europe their own; and exchanged goods in many other areas of the known world while discovering some previously unknown.

"Part of the draw to the Vikings is that for this moment in time, as long as you have a bit of daring and luck, everything seems possible," says Brownworth. "They come crashing into these very controlled states and decaying worlds.... They really should have conquered all of it, given that this was a time where extraordinary individuals had the chance to rise."

The maps detailing their territories do suggest they did an impressive job, even with their habit of taking on the best of what their raided cultures had to offer. The fact is, for three centuries, it was a Viking world and everybody else just lived in it. Here's how it all looked from the blue-sky view.

TESTING THE WATERS
The Early Viking Raids in Europe From 780–814

The Danes came first, arriving on the Isle of Portland in the English Channel in 789. Mistaken for traders and asked to pay a tax, those aboard killed a British official and sailed off. By then the Vikings had traveled European waters for years, sussing out possibilities for plunder.

The Norse attack in Lindisfarne four years later was wholly different: a well-planned and executed, deliberate, strategic marauding of a revered spot in England. It would set the tone for the Viking Age that resonated in vicious, violent attacks, setting Europe and other continents back on their heels.

For those first two decades, the Norsemen and

the Danes made frequent onslaughts on English shores, and brought their forces farther south as well, to the west coast of France, where more gold and precious booty lay in a monastery west of Nantes, before heading south again toward the Bay of Biscayne. At Nantes, as Anders Winroth writes in *The Age of Vikings*, the monks "barricaded the doors and anxiously waited. Resorting to their only remaining hope, they implored God for delivery and salvation.... It did not help."

England With Danelaw Territory, 878

For several decades in the early ninth century, the Vikings concentrated their efforts on Ireland and Scotland, although England, with its poorly run territories, always lay in their sights. In 865, groups of Danes joined for an attack on East Anglia, with Great Heathen Army troops led by Ivar the Boneless and Halfdan Ragnarsson working their way through Northumbria and into York. By 875, reinforcements were strong enough that the Heathen Army split, with each half

seeking lands north and south. Within a few years, the Danelaw territories took up areas in northern and eastern England, extending Viking rule over the people. By 886, the treaty between Alfred the Great, ruler of Wessex, and Guthrum, Viking ruler of East Anglia, created the peace and set some boundaries (this after Alfred's troops defeated Guthrum's in battle, with the latter then promising to convert to Christianity as part payment). But it would always be an uneasy peace, as the clash of cultures, lack of trust and the buildup of British troops set everybody on edge.

Scandinavian Territories in the Viking Age

As far north as Greenland (and then west to the New World beyond) and as far south as Africa, the Vikings established routes of trade—and routs of plenty. From home bases in Norway and Denmark, they made their influence felt in port cities and moved inland when they had to in order to solidify their rule. Even if Greenland and Iceland become

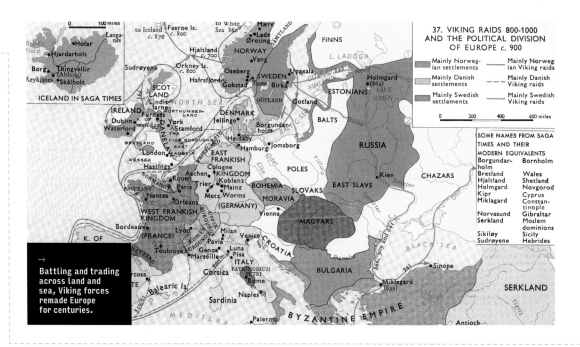

→ Battling and trading across land and sea, Viking forces remade Europe for centuries.

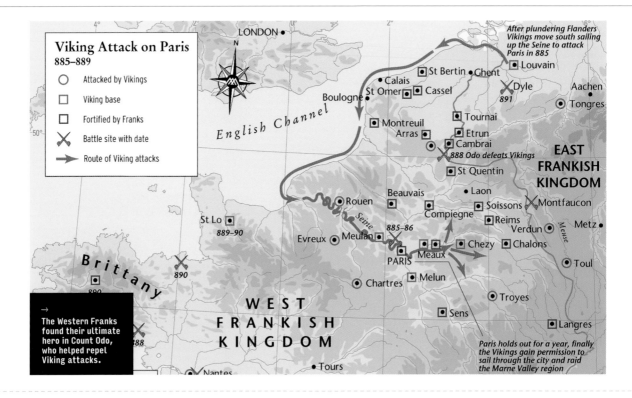

Viking Attack on Paris
885–889

○ Attacked by Vikings

▢ Viking base

▢ Fortified by Franks

✕ Battle site with date

→ Route of Viking attacks

After plundering Flanders Vikings move south sailing up the Seine to attack Paris in 885

888 Odo defeats Vikings

EAST FRANKISH KINGDOM

WEST FRANKISH KINGDOM

Brittany

→ The Western Franks found their ultimate hero in Count Odo, who helped repel Viking attacks.

Paris holds out for a year, finally the Vikings gain permission to sail through the city and raid the Marne Valley region

the definitive territories for their established roots, the way they remade the map, the economy and the cultural structures of Europe for a stretch of centuries still astounds. But another truth comes from the cultural exchange: The Vikings themselves were remade by the civilizations with which they came into contact. "The Viking Age was a moment of great cultural, religious and political achievement," Anders Winroth writes in *The Age of the Vikings*. "Intense Scandinavian contact with Europe unleashed not only the 'fury of the Northmen' onto their European victims, but also a battery of European cultural and political influences on Scandinavia."

FRANKLY SPEAKING
The Vikings Attempt to Raid Paris, 885–889

The Vikings, much like the Mafia in *The Godfather*, were fond of making you an offer you couldn't refuse. It usually amounted to a large sum

payment...or an even costlier, protracted battle. Starting in 840 and for close to 50 years, Paris was under the greedy watch of the Vikings, a great distraction for the West Frank rulers. When the Vikings conducted their Paris siege in 885 after successfully heading through Flanders and past the Seine, Francia's Count Odo—inspired by the fearful notion that the loss of Paris could spell the

→ Invited to bring order to the region, Rurik came, took over Novgorod and ruled Kievan Rus.

end of France—refused to pay up to the Sigfrid-led Dane invaders. Thousands of Viking warriors hit the fortifications surrounding Paris, but Odo, with only 200 soldiers at the time, used a sticky mixture of hot wax and pitch to stop them from scaling the city walls, along with his calls of encouragement to the men to keep the Vikings at bay. In all, the siege lasted eight months, with Odo valiantly sneaking out to procure reinforcements and many more joining the fight on both sides. In the end, Sigfrid accepted a much smaller tribute of silver and Odo's heroic legend was secured in 888: With the death of Charles the Fat, Odo, the "savior of Paris," rose to take the throne.

The Russian Trade Routes of the Varangians

To the European peoples, they were known as Vikings. To the Greeks, however, and to those a little farther north, in the territory now known as Russia, Belarus and Ukraine, they were the Varangians, the trading and pirating forces who worked their territories north of the Black Sea. Rurik, the Varangian chieftain, built Novgorod after settling in the area in 862, beginning a dynasty that would transform the entire region.

At the time, the alluring wealth of Constantinople, capital of the Byzantine Empire, led to a series of wars, creating advantageous trade treaties for the Varangians, who saw tremendous financial advantage through connecting Europe to the riches

of the Arabian and Byzantine territories. The Volga, Dnieper and Dniester routes were broad and lucrative indeed, and the success here, as elsewhere, was astonishing. And then, yet again, these Vikings in time came to accept Christ as their savior and, after the Viking age ended in the late 11th century, the Varangians that remained assimilated and simply became a part of the local culture.

MAP QUEST
Leif Erikson Finds a New World in the 11th Century

Is the original Vinland Map—a Medieval-era world map that was discovered in 1957 and claims to show the Norse path to North America 500 years prior to Columbus—the real deal? Through the years, the map's authenticity has continued to spark controversy and further study. Everything—from the age of its ink to the positions of its boundary lines—has been questioned and examined.

What has generally been accepted, however, is explorer Leif Erikson's actual sailing route from Greenland to Newfoundland, especially given the discovery of Leif's settlement at L'Anse aux Meadows in 1960. As Robert Ferguson writes in *The Vikings: A History*, "About a third of the 150 radio-carbon dates for the L'Anse aux Meadows site are connected to the period of Norse settlement there, dating it between 980 and 1020." Another fact we know: Columbus read the two Norse sagas related to Leif's adventures before heading out to find what he'd believed to be India.

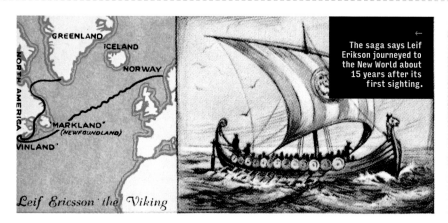

GREENLAND
ICELAND
NORWAY
NORTH AMERICA
MARKLAND
(NEWFOUNDLAND)
VINLAND

The saga says Leif Erikson journeyed to the New World about 15 years after its first sighting.

Leif Ericsson the Viking

"Famous Voyages"
LEIF ERICSSON THE VIKING
Icelandic records tell us that in A.D. 987 Norsemen sailing from Greenland sighted America. In A.D 1000-1002 Leif Ericsson discovered "Helluland" (perhaps Labrador) and "Vinland" (probably Nova Scotia), where Vikings subsequently endeavoured to found a colony, but in vain. There are reports of other journeys to America in 1121 and in 1347.
Ty.phoo Series of 25   No. 3

CHAPTER 2

THEIR NAMES RANG OUT IN FAME

MEET THE FIERCE EXPLORERS AND
WANDERING WARRIORS WHO DEFINED
THE VIKING ERA—ALONG WITH THE
FABLED GODS AND GODDESSES THEY
WORSHIPPED AND RELIED ON TO
GUIDE THEM ON THEIR WAY.

↓
Canute the Great ruled the mighty North Sea Empire, but in Viking lore, he's best known for not stopping the tide.

THE NORSE FORCE

THE GREATEST VIKINGS RAIDED, ROBBED AND
RULED FOR CENTURIES. HERE ARE THE 10 MOST
SPECTACULAR FIGURES FROM THE AGE.

In the series *Vikings*, Clive Standen plays Rollo as ruthless, skilled and jealous.

ROLLO

TIME CAPSULE
Rollo lived from approximately 860–930 and rose to become the first ruler of the land of the Norse—aka Normandy—in northern France.

THE FACT SHEET
After years of sea battles, Rollo raided the area around the Seine and held it. French King Charles the Simple (so called because he always got right to the point), realizing he had no way of pushing the Vikings out, offered up the Treaty of Saint Clair-sur-Epte, which Rollo signed. It effectively guaranteed Rollo his kingdom (and the chance to pillage in nearby lands) if he agreed to protect the coastline (and, farther down the road, Paris) from other Viking raids and provide military aid. In exchange, Rollo and his entire army would have to become Christians. The agreement worked for all concerned, and Rollo eventually adopted many French ways of living and fighting, while also restoring a slew of churches. One of his famed descendants: William the Conqueror.

FROM THE OFT-TOLD SAGAS
His entire life prior to the treaty is shrouded in legend. Was he born in Norway or Denmark? It's an ugly point of contention; different sagas make warring claims. He's regarded as having an aristocratic upbringing, and some believe he counts a family connection to Scottish island King Ketill Flatnose. In 885, at the supposed height of his plundering glory, he may have been part of a huge raid on Paris, consisting of 700 ships and 40,000 men. Oh, yes—and the baptism of all Rollo's men didn't go without controversy: The traditional kissing of the king's foot, a duty Rollo delegated to one of his angry subordinates, ended with the king being kicked onto his butt. The events after the baptism didn't quite go as planned either; when Charles was captured in battle and forced to give up his throne, Rollo considered the pact to be null and void—and went back to raiding.

THE CRAZIEST CLAIMS
It has been suggested that Rollo's family had fallen out with warrior Eric Bloodaxe, who hacked the youthful Rollo's brother to death and forced Rollo into exile. That may have paved the way for the nickname "Rollo the Walker," although he was also supposed to be so huge in stature that no horse could support him. Now *that's* big.

ROLLO—IN DENMARK

CANUTE THE GREAT

↑
With his feet set firmly in the tide, Canute indicates that secular control can never be as strong as nature.

TIME CAPSULE
Born around 990 and died November 12, 1035, Canute the Great was the ultimate empire builder.

THE FACT SHEET
Canute Sweynsson was the son of Denmark's King Sweyn Forkbeard and grandson of fellow Scandinavian ruler Harald Bluetooth, but he earned his "great" suffix through victory and rule. After helping his dad conquer England in 1013, he saw it fall away from him when Sweyn died a year later and the people elevated the exiled Anglo-Saxon King Æthelred the Unready back to the throne. Two years later, Æthelred was dead and his son Edmund Ironside succeeded him, setting up a battle royal for the ages, which Canute won. The treaty that followed (along with Edmund's death) gave Canute rule over all of England. Marrying Æthelred's widow also didn't hurt his unification efforts. When Canute's brother Harald died two years later, Canute rose to take Harald's place atop the throne of Denmark (whether the people wanted him to or not). When he also conquered Norway in 1028, he became ruler of the North Sea empire (he eventually added part of Sweden to his holdings as well). While violence, or the threat of it, was always present, Canute's ability to adapt to the wide range of cultures and unite the people with stability made his legend.

FROM THE OFT-TOLD SAGAS
As is the case with so many a Viking, the truth about Canute's life before his father's invasion of England—including his birth or even the name of his mother—is as murky as the seas. He also apparently didn't suffer fools, among them the Saxon rivals who defected to his side in a battle for the English throne; once won, he supposedly had them executed for their too-fickle nature. His rule was said to be marked by a tidy mix of wealth and brutality—that, and his many lovers beyond his wife, seemed to make for a somewhat uneasy bond with the Christian church.

THE CRAZIEST CLAIMS
The tale of "King Canute and the Tide" has falsely become something of an "Emperor's New Clothes" story. Some say he is portrayed as a nutty monarch who tries to show his fawning staff that he has the power to control the sea itself. In fact, the story is about Canute showing he *can't* "stop the tide," and that only God can do so.

TIME CAPSULE

Erik Thorvaldsson, who lived approximately from 950–1003, was an explorer who founded the first settlement in Greenland.

THE FACT SHEET

Was it his hair color or hair-trigger temper that earned him the nickname The Red? It could certainly have been both, and the latter ran in the family, as a murder committed by his father, Thorvald Asvaldsson, led the clan to run from Erik's native Norway to Iceland. Erik himself

→
It was during his exile that Erik embraced a life of exploration, leading him to Greenland.

was accused of manslaughter in 982 and fled, sailing to a vast arctic land he discovered and chose to name it Greenland because, as *The Saga of Erik the Red* later put it, "people would be much more tempted to go there if it had an attractive name." The Middle Ages marketing pitch worked: Returning to Iceland later on, he sailed back with 25 vessels to Greenland and those on the 14 that survived the journey made their home there. (A little global warming at the time actually gave the claim a tad more validity.) Erik died not long after declining to accompany his son Leif Erikson on his voyage to North America. An epidemic brought to Greenland by a settler eventually killed Erik.

FROM THE OFT-TOLD SAGAS

Was Erik's union with his wife, Thjodhild, troubled by religious differences? The sagas make a bit of hay about Thjodhild's embracing Christianity and Erik's reluctance to give up his heathen ways, claiming that her faith "annoyed him greatly"—perhaps because she refused to go to bed with a heathen. She also wouldn't live with him after her conversion, and a church built near the homestead was a standing reminder of the rift in their marriage.

THE CRAZIEST CLAIMS

What exactly was a Thing? It was a legal assembly meant to settle a dispute. At one such Thing in Iceland, Erik was accused of killing several slaves, followed by a neighbor, Eyjolf Sauer, and another man; the manslaughter charges ended up deciding his fate. He was sentenced to what was called the Lesser Outlawry, which included a fine and a three-year exile. But after another incident involving more killings in Iceland, his punishment was upped to the Full Outlawry, and he fled to the world he came to name Greenland.

ERIK THE RED

→ Olaf battled for riches and rule, but he was equally relentless in spreading the word of Christ to the people.

OLAF TRYGGVASON

TIME CAPSULE

Born in, perhaps, the mid-960s, and perishing in a valiant battle on September 9, 1000 (or so they say), Olaf Tryggvason ruled Norway and brought the word of Jesus along with him.

THE FACT SHEET

Viking lore is filled with figures that transformed from marauders into missionaries, and Olaf may be chief among them. His origins, told almost exclusively through the sagas, have a biblical sensibility. After the murder of his royal father, his pregnant mother escaped to Scotland's Orkney Islands, where she gave birth to Olaf and set him on a path of familial vengeance. His young adulthood teemed with murderous actions, raiding and plundering, along with a marriage to Queen Geira of the Germanic area of Wendland. Her early death led to even *more* plundering, followed, some say, by his conversion to Christianity, with the voice of God reaching him one night, beginning with the words, "Hear me, you who promise to be a good man." In 995, he traveled to Norway upon hearing that King Haakon had lost the support of the people; he took the throne and reigned for several years, making sure everybody was baptized whether they wanted to be or not. But ambition ruled his heart and when he was set to lose the naval Battle of Svolder in the Baltic Sea, he leapt overboard to his death.

FROM THE OFT-TOLD SAGAS

In the early and mid-990s, say the sagas, Olaf's alliance with Sweyn Forkbeard found them plundering England together in the Battle of Maldon, until King Æthelred paid them £16,000 in silver in the hope they'd stop and instead agree to protect English interests. Their bond was broken a few years later in part from Olaf's controversial marriage to Sweyn's sister Tyra, who'd left her husband against Sweyn's wishes. Sweyn was among those supposedly on the large number of ships that outnumbered Olaf's in his final battle.

THE CRAZIEST CLAIMS

Beyond the assertion that Olaf survived that jump overboard, it was said that he forced people to convert to Christianity using some exceedingly violent methods. And really, if someone was set to pry your mouth open and insert a snake, or put a load of hot coals on your belly if you didn't accept Christ into your heart, you'd say "Amen" pretty quick.

KING OLAF

A KINGLY COIN

LEIF ERIKSON

TIME CAPSULE

Born sometime in the 970s and died in the 1020s, Lief Erikson famously beat Columbus to North America by a good 500 years.

THE FACT SHEET

This son of Erik the Red was said to have been born in Iceland, and like many explorers, made some of his greatest discoveries after being blown off course. (Indeed, the Viking Naddodd had discovered Iceland that way.) Heading back to Iceland from Greenland, Erik was steered by the wind instead to Norway, where King Olaf Tryggvason swore him to the word of Christ. Years later, hearing of a lush land sighted by a merchant named Bjarni Herjólfsson (who'd found it after being blown off course), Leif took Bjarni's reverse route and made land on what are now several Canadian territories. He named the area, including Newfoundland and New Brunswick, Vinland, because of its richness in grapes and many berries (and, like his dad, he felt that a good name would bring more settlers). After spending the winter, he headed back to Greenland with a cargo full of grapes and loads of timber, opening up a potentially lucrative trade route. But he remained in Greenland after this first voyage, and his brother Thorvald and sister Freydís explored the territory further. His death remains unknown.

FROM THE OFT-TOLD SAGAS

The Saga of the Greenlanders and *The Saga of Erik the Red* give us the most "information" about the life of a man considered handsome, stalwart and wise. Originally, his father Erik was expected to lead the expedition to what became known as Vinland, but riding toward the ship on his horse, Erik fell off—a very bad omen—and declared he was not fated to discover another land.

LEIF STANDS TALL IN ICELAND

THE CRAZIEST CLAIMS

Some scholars believe *The Saga of Erik the Red* suggests Thorfinn Karlsefni and his wife, Gudrid, are the real discoverers of the New World, with Leif a kind of accidental tourist. However, those claims seem to be tied to an attempt to get one of Thorfinn's descendants a much greater degree of renown. Either way, it didn't stop President Calvin Coolidge in 1925 from declaring that Leif came to the continent first. Need more "proof"? There are lots of Leif statues throughout America. The one of Thorfinn installed in Philadelphia in 1920 was knocked down by vandals in 2018 and dragged into the Schuylkill River.

→ *The Landing of the Vikings* is said to depict Leif's journey—albeit with wings that were never on his helmet.

One saga suggests Aslaug first refused Ragnar's hand until he had won the day in Normandy.

TIME CAPSULE

Relentless ransacker Ragnar Lothbrok lived during the early to mid-ninth century and was the quintessential Norse warrior of legend.

THE FACT SHEET

Was Ragnar a man or a myth? Common dude or demigod? A figure from the days of yore or a star from the tales of lore? The answer is a resounding "Yes!" Nothing is known of his birth and one tale of his death is a real humdinger. What we believe we know of Ragnar is that he was the first Scandinavian to invade Britain, but was an even bigger thorn in the side of Medieval France since he led the siege of Paris in 845. To teach French King Charles the Bald not to mess with him, he hung 111 French prisoners in full view of the royal to please the god Odin. He was also involved in the first instance of "Danegeld," in which kings paid Vikings a lot of money to leave them alone. The other proof of Ragnar's existence comes with the Great Heathen Army, led by four of his sons—including legendary historical figures Ivar the Boneless and Björn Ironside—who invaded England to avenge Ragnar's death.

FROM THE OFT-TOLD SAGAS

Among Ragnar's wives was the gorgeous Princess Aslaug, a woman the stories say was so beautiful, the bakers would let their bread burn while staring at her. But to win his first wife, Ragnar crafted his Lothbrok, meaning "hairy breeches"—the strange sand-covered leather leggings he prepared to help him slay a dragon or giant serpent (by keeping the creature from biting him) to earn her hand.

THE CRAZIEST CLAIMS

The popular TV series *Vikings* does Ragnar (Travis Fimmel played the role) no favors in the nonfiction department, though it elevated him to star status. The series makes him seem ageless (he wasn't), a brother to Rollo (not possible) and Christian (um…no). But the nuttiest claim is that Ragnar was killed by British King Ælla, who lowered him into a pit of deadly vipers. Ragnar supposedly suggested that his sons would avenge him, and legend has it the Great Heathen Army killed Ælla using what the sagas call "the Blood Eagle." This prolonged torture is said to begin with the ritual removal of your lungs through your back, to give you "wings," followed by a little disemboweling. Needless to say, Viking lore sure had a taste for torment.

TRAVIS FIMMEL AS RAGNAR

RAGNAR LOTHBROK

Both sagas that mention Freydís characterize her as strong-willed and a match for any man.

FREYDÍS EIRÍKSDÓTTIR

TIME CAPSULE

Born around 970, her death remains a mystery, and Freydís Eiríksdóttir is regarded as the great warrior-goddess of the New World expedition.

THE FACT SHEET

Those pesky sagas offered a "You say to-*may*-to and I say to-*mah*-to" view of the pagan princess who scared the bejesus out of the native Vinland peoples. In *The Saga of Erik the Red*, named for Freydís' father, she was cited for bravery that made her more than a match for any man. Having followed her brother Leif Erikson's lead and traveled to the established New World settlement of Vinland, she and her expedition were attacked by the bitter local Skræling—a Norse pejorative word for the Native Americans that could be translated to mean anything from "barbarian" to "weakling." When her Viking men retreated, the bitterly determined Freydís, believed to be eight months pregnant at the time, shouted, "Why run you away from such worthless creatures, stout men that ye are, when, as seems to me likely you might slaughter them like so many cattle? Give me a weapon! I know I could fight better than any of you." Lifting a sword, she began to strip away her garments and beat the sword against her exposed breast, spooking the enemy into full retreat.

FROM THE OFT-TOLD SAGAS

Or there's *The Saga of the Greenlanders* take, which may have been motivated to quibble with the very unchristian idea of a powerful woman warrior. In that story, Freydís traveled to Vinland in partnership with two brothers whom she first deceived by bringing along more soldiers than they did, before banishing them to lesser quarters, and finally—after goading her husband by telling him the pair beat her—got them and their men killed.

THE CRAZIEST CLAIMS

Adding insult to *Saga of the Greenlanders* injury, it was noted that Freydís' husband refused to kill the five women in the brothers' party...so Freydís grabbed an ax and massacred them herself. Hoping to keep all this secret, she threatened to kill anyone who spoke of it. When her brother Leif ultimately did hear of it, he predicted that Freydís' descendants would suffer by being looked down upon forever, which the saga suggests was the case. Sounds more like a Middle Ages gender-based cautionary tale this glass-ceiling buster hardly deserved.

ALICIA AGNESON PLAYS FREYDÍS IN *VIKINGS*

EGIL SKALLAGRÍMSSON

TIME CAPSULE
Born around 904 and died around 995, Egil Skallagrímsson wore the mantle of warrior-poet.

THE FACT SHEET
As one historian sums it up, "Like his father, Egil was black-haired and ugly," while another describes him as "the poet, warrior, drunkard, killer and eponymous hero of *Egil's Saga*." Speculation is that Egil had Paget's disease, which causes bone deformities that, in his case, increased the size of his skull. Viking saga translation: His head could repel blows from an ax. That didn't stop him from testing an ax blade's sharpness on the heads of others, beginning at age 7, when he attacked a local boy who'd cheated him in a game. And it was said he killed a man by biting through his neck. But he also began writing poems at age 3, displaying a talent that served him beyond his berserking; his keen reading of runestones was also renowned. His wild temper, which put him constantly at odds with Norway's Viking King Eric Bloodaxe and his queen Gunnhild, also helped him win a battle for English King Athelstan that cost the life of his beloved brother. Egil spent the victory feast seething…until the king, understanding the moment, extended a large golden ring on the end of his sword, which Egil took on his own sword. That ended that.

FROM THE OFT-TOLD SAGAS
The battle with Eric Bloodaxe nearly cost Egil his life. Captured while sailing past Northumbria, Egil was brought before Eric and sentenced to die. He composed a poem to soothe his enemy's anger, but was rebuffed, and told he'd be killed in the morning.

That night, Egil wrote a *much* more elaborate set of verses and recited them to Eric, praising the man's incredible exploits, using metaphors and writing skills that ultimately won Egil freedom. The poem has come to be called "The Head-Ransom."

THE CRAZIEST CLAIMS
News from the sagas is that one night at a gathering, knowing he couldn't drink another drop of mead, Egil pressed his host against a wall, put both hands upon his shoulders and offered a projectile vomit of such force he nearly drowned the man. Clearly, Egil was not fond of moderation on any score.

EGIL DRAWN ON THE PAGES OF A SAGA

FIERCE EGIL CELEBRATED IN NORWAY

Harald felt himself invincible, but the ill-fated 1066 Battle of Stamford Bridge proved him wrong.

TIME CAPSULE

Born sometime around 1015 and died September 25, 1066 (a fateful day in Norse history), Harald Hardrada was the last king of the Viking era.

THE FACT SHEET

Harald's tale plays out like the full arc of the Viking experience, filled with family strife, exile, battles, compromises, outsize ambitions and valiant death. As a teen, he was injured in the Battle of Stiklestad that saw the death of his half brother "Saint" Olaf Haraldsson, who'd been king of Norway. Exiled in Russia, Harald rose to a place of wealth and renown after joining the Byzantine emperor's esteemed Varangian Guard. Returning to make his Scandinavian mark in the 1040s, he joined forces with the man who would be (Danish) King Sweyn Estridsson and plundered in Denmark, attracting the ire of his nephew, Norway and Denmark's King Magnus the Good. Magnus made Harald a deal: Join with me instead and I'll make you co-ruler. A year later, Magnus died, and Harald ruled Norway, while Sweyn took over Denmark. Harald and Sweyn battled for years

(Hardrada meant "hard ruler") until a 1064 pact. Then Harald set his sights on England, which he invaded in 1066, and celebrated a great victory... for all of two days, until England's King Harold Godwinson overwhelmed Harald and his troops in the last great Viking battle.

FROM THE OFT-TOLD SAGAS

If we're to believe 12th-century Icelandic historian Snorri Sturluson, Harald had the kind of profile that would have made him quite popular with women. Physically "larger than other men and stronger" (between 6 and 7 feet) with big hands and feet, Harald was a whiz at skaldic poetry and a master of brewing, horse riding, skiing, shooting, rowing and harp playing. He's a catch, all right.

THE CRAZIEST CLAIMS

The 2006 David Gibbons historical novel *Crusader Gold* puts Harald into an Indiana Jones–like adventure, suggesting he may have taken the golden menorah of the ancient Jerusalem temple with him on an exploration to the New World. That's another claim—that Harald sought to rediscover the Vinland Leif Erikson had found.

HARALD HARDRADA

TIME CAPSULE

In the late 10th century, Icelandic warrior Gunnar Hámundarson inspired courageous tales in one of the most revered sagas of the Middle Ages.

THE FACT SHEET

Are there any facts whatsoever about his existence? Nope. But among the greatest "facts" of Viking lore is that the sagas provide lessons that have guided historical views and perspectives for centuries. Gunnar's life is covered in *Njál's Saga*, which speaks to how honor, gender, masculinity, blood feuds, prophesy, Christianity and—in this case—the bond between Gunnar and his closest friend, the lawyer Njáll Þorgeirsson, and the rather complicated relationship their wives maintained shaped the lore.

FROM THE OFT-TOLD SAGAS

The description of Gunnar is so flattering, one would think the unknown author was his mom. He is called tall, strong and so ambidextrous with his swords that when smiting with them, "three seemed to flash through the air at once." Perhaps most astonishingly, he can leap more than his own height with all his armor on. He swims like a seal, is unbeatable in any sport, fair-skinned, blue-eyed, ruddy-cheeked, invincible in battle (and there are many), sturdy-framed—and he sports a mane of blond curls. His weapon of choice? A magical pole-arm spear called an atgeir that he used to stab victims in the air. Oh, and he can hit you between the eyes with a rock. Njáll warns him never to kill two members of any one family, which will spell his poor fate. So, needless to say…

THE CRAZIEST CLAIMS

This is where Gunnar's wife, Hallgerda, comes in. Gunnar is her third husband; the previous two were each killed after she'd provoked them into striking her. ("I am said to be hard to please in husbands," she deadpans at one point.) Njáll warns him against the union but lust wins out, and epic bitterness between Njáll's wife, Bergthora, and Hallgerda leads to much killing, resulting in Gunnar's banishment for three years. Vengeance is sought and Gunnar is winning—that is, until his archer's bowstring breaks. He asks Hallgerda for a lock of her hair as replacement; she refuses (they'd argued prior when she stole food during a famine, and he stupidly struck her), and in hand-to-hand combat, Gunnar is killed. As happens in the sagas all too often, the strong woman proves the heroic man's undoing.

GUNNAR HÁMUNDARSON

PENGUIN CLASSICS
NJAL'S SAGA

THE "TRUE" SOURCE OF GUNNAR'S LIFE

←
Gunnar liked his weapons, although none proved as valuable as his piercing atgeir.

THEY WALKED TALL

VIKING HISTORY LEAVES ROOM FOR PLENTY OF STAR STORIES, AND THESE ARE 20 MORE THAT SHAPED THE LORE.

AUD THE DEEP-MINDED
The strong-willed and noble queen of Dublin (and wife of King Olaf) captained a ship to Orkney in the Scottish Islands and established a dynasty there. She was given a traditional Viking ship burial upon her death.

BJÖRN IRONSIDE
Son of Ragnar Lothbrok and part of the Great Heathen Army, he raided the Mediterranean in 860 alongside his brother Hastein, and was believed to have been the first ruler of the Munsö dynasty in Sweden.

ERIC BLOODAXE
King of Norway, Northumbria and York, this son of Harald Fairhair is regarded as larger than life, but flawed and violent. Among other things, he's known for his long conflict with Egil Skallagrímsson and marriage to Gunnhild.

FLÓKI VILGERDARSON
Nicknamed "Raven" because of his navigational skills (and the ravens he carried to help him), he's the first explorer to intentionally sail to Iceland—and though he didn't think much of the place, he eventually returned and helped feed the need for colonization.

GODFRID
A Danish Viking warlord who reinforced sections of the enormous border wall known as Danevirke, his outsize ambition to rule France and then Germany was undone when he was mysteriously killed by one of his supporters.

GUDRID THORBJARNARDÓTTIR
An intrepid Icelandic explorer who, alongside her husband, Thorfinn Karlsefni, led an expedition to Vinland in the New World. Their son Snorri Thorfinnsson became the first European born in North America.

OLAF HARALDSSON
Olaf II of Norway—St. Olaf—became the country's patron saint due to his efforts to convert the people. A symbol of independence, his troops were ultimately outnumbered and he was killed at the Battle of Stiklestad.

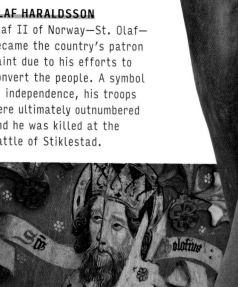

GUDRID

ST. OLAF

THEY WALKED TALL

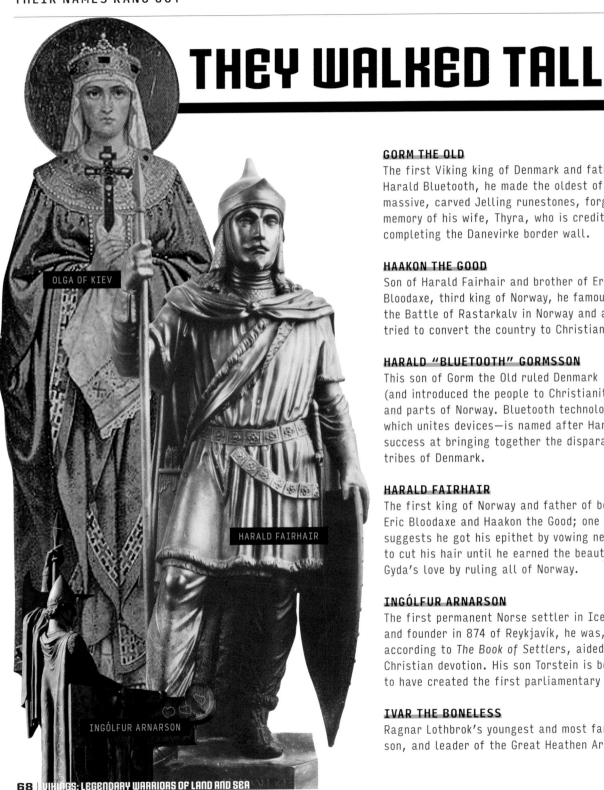

OLGA OF KIEV

HARALD FAIRHAIR

INGÓLFUR ARNARSON

GORM THE OLD
The first Viking king of Denmark and father of Harald Bluetooth, he made the oldest of the massive, carved Jelling runestones, forged in memory of his wife, Thyra, who is credited with completing the Danevirke border wall.

HAAKON THE GOOD
Son of Harald Fairhair and brother of Eric Bloodaxe, third king of Norway, he famously won the Battle of Rastarkalv in Norway and also tried to convert the country to Christianity.

HARALD "BLUETOOTH" GORMSSON
This son of Gorm the Old ruled Denmark (and introduced the people to Christianity) and parts of Norway. Bluetooth technology—which unites devices—is named after Harald's success at bringing together the disparate tribes of Denmark.

HARALD FAIRHAIR
The first king of Norway and father of both Eric Bloodaxe and Haakon the Good; one saga suggests he got his epithet by vowing never to cut his hair until he earned the beautiful Gyda's love by ruling all of Norway.

INGÓLFUR ARNARSON
The first permanent Norse settler in Iceland and founder in 874 of Reykjavík, he was, according to *The Book of Settlers*, aided by his Christian devotion. His son Torstein is believed to have created the first parliamentary Thing.

IVAR THE BONELESS
Ragnar Lothbrok's youngest and most famous son, and leader of the Great Heathen Army

(played by Alex Høgh Andersen, top right, on *Vikings*), he avenged his father's death, raided England and was intriguingly cruel.

MAGNUS THE GOOD

"Magnus, hear a mighty poem!" the court poet Arnórr once began as he extolled the virtues of the king of both Norway and Denmark. His ability to unite the rule was undone after his death.

OLGA OF KIEV

After the death of her husband, Igor I, she ruled Kievan Rus (Russia, Belarus and Ukraine all claim a bond to the place) as a regent for her son. She was elevated to sainthood for trying to spread Christianity in the region.

RURIK THE RUS

He was a Swedish Viking who—according to the *Primary Chronicle* of Kievan Rus—founded the first Norse state in Russia, built the city of Novgorod and fathered the Rurik Dynasty, which led, ultimately, all the way to Tsarist rule.

SITRIC SILKBEARD

The Viking king of Dublin and the final major Norse figure to sit on the throne in Ireland, he raided plenty and ruled for 46 years, even though he had a long-standing reputation as an outsider among the locals.

SWEYN ESTRIDSSON

This grandson of Sweyn Forkbeard and father of five kings was the last Viking ruler of

IVAR THE BONELESS

SWEYN FORKBEARD

Denmark, doing so for almost 30 years beginning in 1047. He was known for feuding with Norway's King Harald Hardrada in a 16-year power struggle.

SWEYN FORKBEARD

Son of Harald Bluetooth (Sweyn famously seized his dad's throne), Viking king of Denmark, raider of England, father of Canute the Great—Sweyn had quite the résumé, but died five weeks after winning control of England on Christmas Day in 1013.

THORGEIR LJOSVETNINGAGODI

He was an Icelandic pagan priest and lawspeaker who, around 1000, was tasked with deciding whether the country should be heathen or Christian. After a full day of silent meditation, he chose the latter—a decision of both practicality and faith.

DAZZLING DEITIES

MEET THE GODS GUIDING THE VIKINGS' WAY.

← Images of Thor's hammer appear on five different runestones in Denmark and Sweden.

THOR

God of thunder, lightning and storms, Thor travels the worlds in an eternal quest to vanquish the giants—the archenemies of the gods—most often using his famed hammer, Mjölnir.

ROYAL RELATIONS Son of Odin and his mistress Jord, a giantess

MOST MEMORABLE MYTH When a giant steals the hammer and demands the goddess Freyja's hand in marriage for its return, Thor disguises himself as the beautiful goddess (a brave, but controversial decision in a society outraged by cross-dressing) and travels to Giantland appearing as the faux fiancée. When the hammer is delivered, Thor destroys the giants in one blow.

MODERN-DAY MATTERS Today, Thor is perhaps the best-known of the Norse gods due to his popular Marvel comic books and movies, the first of which debuted in August 1962.

FRIGG

A powerful sky goddess associated with foresight and wisdom, Frigg is a protector of marriage and is responsible for weaving the clouds. Her realm is the hearth, and she sits at the spinning wheel day after day, aiding her devotees in all domestic needs.

ROYAL RELATIONS Wife of Odin, mother of Baldur

MOST MEMORABLE MYTH When Frigg and Odin fight over which of two warring Germanic

> **"If plague or famine threatens, sacrifices are made to Thor's statue."**
>
> ADAM OF BREMEN

tribes deserve victory, the wise goddess puts her sharp mind to work. The power couple decides to settle their argument the following morning, agreeing that whichever tribe Odin sees first will be granted victory. Odin is sure he'll win, as his chosen victors are visible from his side of the bed. But Frigg, one step ahead of her husband, turns Odin's bed to the opposite side of the wall overnight. Odin awakes and declares Frigg's tribe the victors.

MODERN-DAY MATTERS Friday comes from the Old English Frīgedæg, or "day of Frigg."

→ Frigg, known as Freyia, rode a chariot pulled by two male cats, Bygul and Trjegul.

Associated with the horse cult, Freyr's own equine was called Blóðughófi, or Bloody Hoof.

FREYR

Freyr is one of the most popular and respected of the Norse gods, even called "the foremost of the gods" in an Old Norse poem. Freyr is associated with the weather, royalty, human sexuality and agriculture.

ROYAL RELATIONS Brother to Freyja, son of Njörd

SIGNATURE SYMBOL Freyr was rarely spotted without his ship, *Skíðblaðnir*, which caught an eternally favorable sail and, with Mary Poppins-style magic, could fold up into a small bag.

MOST MEMORABLE MYTH Freyr controlled the prosperity and destiny of many with his benevolence, handling fertility, the harvest and peace. When his signature chariot arrived in a village, the townspeople would lay down their arms and revel in a festive period of peace and joy.

BRAGI

The god of poetry and music, his name literally translates to "poet" from the Viking word "bragr" or "poetr." With a long beard and runes often carved on his tongue, his creativity eclipses that of all other gods.

ROYAL RELATIONS Son of Odin and the giantess Gunnlod; husband to Idun

MOST MEMORABLE MYTH As peacekeeper and deliverer of light, Bragi is allowed to wander the Nine Worlds freely, bringing music and joy to the inhabitants and leaving each with a sense of wonder and cooperation.

ODIN

A seeker of wisdom, Odin is a god wrapped in contradictions: He's both the god of justice and of trickery, of poetry and of war.

ROYAL RELATIONS Husband of the goddess Frigg

SIGNATURE SYMBOL Two ravens, Huginn and Muninn, sit on his shoulders, bringing news from other worlds before breakfast.

MOST MEMORABLE MYTH In his unrelenting quest for wisdom, Odin once ventured to the well where Mimir, a shadowy being with unparalleled intelligence, resided. Much of Mimir's cosmic knowledge came from drinking from the well, and when Odin requested a sip, Mimir demanded his eye in return. Odin gouged out one eye and dropped it into the well, and in exchange Mimir filled Odin's horn, offering the god a swig.

↓
Odin is referred to as the "raven god," the "raven tempter" and the "priest of the raven sacrifice."

←
In the Prose Edda, Bragi is revered "most of all for fluency of speech and skill with words."

NJÖRD

A god of the sea, Njörd is associated with ships and seafaring, calming storms, aiding distressed boats and sending favorable winds to sailors.

ROYAL RELATIONS Father of Freyr and Freyja

MOST MEMORABLE MYTH When the giantess Skadi arrived in Aesir seeking revenge for the slaying of her father, the gods settled, offering her any god she desired as her husband. Skadi mistakenly selects Njörd, believing him to be Baldur, leading to a short and unpleasant marriage between the incompatible pair. Splitting their time between Skadi's snowy home in the mountains and Njörd's beach house, neither could stand the other's lifestyle, and the two parted amicably.

MODERN-DAY MATTERS The popular Norse saying, "As rich as Njörd," harkens to his role as a fertility god, capable of bestowing good fortune.

→ Through the 19th century, Norse folk would thank the god of the sea for the fish at their table.

BALDUR

Baldur is so full of goodness, graciousness and cheer that he is often depicted as giving off actual light.

ROYAL RELATIONS Son of Odin and Frigg; husband of the goddess Nanna and father of the god Forseti

MOST MEMORABLE MYTH After Baldur dreams of his death, Frigg secures an oath from all the world not to harm her son. The gods throw weapons and random objects at Baldur, amused by his invincibility. But Loki, learning Baldur is still vulnerable to a sprig of mistletoe, makes a spear from the plant. When Baldur's brother Hodr uses the weapon, Baldur dies instantly.

→ Frigg deemed mistletoe too small and innocent to require an oath.

→ Gefjon is featured as the allegorical mother of Scandinavia in the 19th-century book *A Poem in Four Cantos*.

GEFJON

Though a minor goddess herself, Gefjon is associated with virginity, agriculture and plowing.

MOST MEMORABLE MYTH After disguising herself as a beggar woman, she asks the king of Sweden to give her land. When the king tells Gefjon she can have as much land as she can plow in one day and one night, she takes to the western part of Sweden—a flat, fertile area—and uses her oxen sons to plow so deep they cut out a huge part of the land, creating a new island that is dubbed Zealand.

MODERN-DAY MATTERS Today, Zealand remains a large, inhabited island off Denmark's coast.

FORSETI

Beings far and wide travel to see Forseti—who resides in Glitnir, the Hall of Justice—seeking mediation for their problems. No one, it's said, is dissatisfied by Forseti's noble and fair judgments.

ROYAL RELATIONS Son of Baldur and the goddess Nanna

SIGNATURE SYMBOL The ax

MOST MEMORABLE MYTH A younger god of Norse mythology, Forseti chooses justice over vengeance in reverence for his father—the most famous murder victim of their time. He approaches each wrongdoing with logic and fairness, without the telltale impulsiveness of so many gods before him.

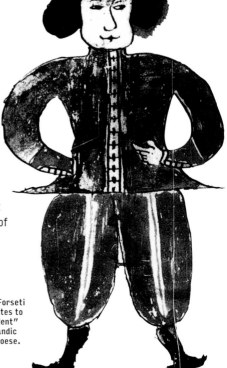

→ Today, Forseti translates to "president" in Icelandic and Faroese.

→
The siblings were endlessly pursued by the fierce wolves Sköll and Hati, who sought to darken the world.

SÓL & MÁNI

First emerging with the creation of the cosmos, the siblings personify the sun and the moon.

ROYAL RELATIONS The sister–brother pair are the children of a giant named Mundilfari.

MOST MEMORABLE MYTH The gods came together to create different parts of the day and year, along with the phases of the moon, so that both Sól and Máni had a place in the new world.

IDUN

Belonging to the Aesir tribe of deities, Idun is known as "the rejuvenating one." She is a goddess associated with fruits— particularly apples—and youth.

ROYAL RELATIONS Wife of Bragi

MOST MEMORABLE MYTH In one of the best-known Norse tales, Idun is famously kidnapped while watching over the fruit that provides gods with eternal youth. When Loki convinces Idun that he has found more magical fruits in a forest outside of Asgard, she follows him with her own apples, seeking a comparison to the newfound fruit, but is instead led right into the home of the giant Thjazi. When the gods and goddesses begin going gray, quickly feeling the effects of old age, they discover Loki's deception and set out to save the goddess.

→
In the poem "Hrafnagaldr Óðins," we learn Idun was descended from elves.

→ Ullr is often depicted holding a bow and standing on skis.

"[Ullr] is such a good archer and ski-runner that no one can rival him."

GYLFAGINNING IN *THE PROSE EDDA,* TRANSLATED BY JEAN I. YOUNG

ULLR

Not much is known of Ullr, but his aptitude for skiing, hunting and archery is well-documented.

ROYAL RELATIONS Son of Sif, the grain goddess, and stepson of Thor

MOST MEMORABLE MYTH Most of Ullr's stories have been lost, but experts believe there was a tale of him traveling the ocean on top of a shield.

MODERN-DAY MATTERS Today, skiers the world over look to Ullr for favorable conditions on the slopes. They pray to Ullr when there's a lack of snow and cheer the god's generosity when a blizzard hits.

CHAPTER 3

HOW VIKINGS TRAVELED AND TRADED

WITH THEIR SWIFT SHIPS AND SENSE
OF ADVENTURE (NOT TO MENTION
A PASSION FOR PLUNDER), THE
EARLY SCANDINAVIANS DISCOVERED
NEW WORLDS, BOOSTED ECONOMIES
AND SAILED INTO HISTORY.

SAILS OF THE

THE VIKING AGE TRULY BEGAN WHEN SCANDINAVIA BIRTHED
THE MOST POWERFUL SYMBOL OF THE DAY: THE MIGHTY SHIPS.

The poets sing of them in the sagas. They are long and lithe of body but terrible of purpose. Indeed, nothing is so powerful as the marauding grace of the Vikings' fighting longships. This, from *The Saga of Harald Hardrada*: "Then Harald and Sweyn fitted out ships and gathered together a great force; and when the troops were ready they sailed from the East towards Denmark.... So says Valgard: 'Harald! thou hast the isle laid waste/ The Seeland men away hast chased/And the wild wolf by daylight roams/Through their deserted silent homes....'"

And in *The Saga of Magnus the Good*, these words of honor and warning: "Now in this strophe, royal youth!/I tell no more than the plain truth/ Thy armed outfit from the strand/Left many a keel-trace on the sand/And never did a king before/ So many ships to any shore/Lead on, as thou to Vindland's isle:/The Vindland men in fright recoil."

There's little doubt enemies *did* recoil. It's difficult to imagine a sight more frightening than the coming dragonhead, front and center on the prow of an oaken longship, propelled swiftly through the ocean on a mission of menace. Without the invention of these ships, there would have been no Viking Age worth speaking of.

By the same token, few ships seem more miraculous than Viking trading vessels, some of which could carry as much as 60 metric tons of men and materials, animals and goods.

The ships of the Norse and the Danes so perfectly represented the evolution of the Vikings from world-beaters to world-makers, and the discovery of actual ships over the past several decades represents some of the most astounding buried treasure archaeologists have ever found. The vision of these vessels skirting through the seas seems ready made for pounding orchestral accompaniment.

As the author Sarah Orne Jewett wrote in her 1887 book *The Normans*, "In the Southern countries there had always been rude castles in which the people could shelter themselves, but the Northmen could build no castles that a torch could not destroy. They trusted much more to their ships than to their houses, and some of their great captains disdained to live on shore at all.... When we picture the famous sea-kings' ships to ourselves, we do not wonder that the Northmen were so proud of them, or that the skalds were never tired of recounting their glories."

The Vikings created a number of vessels large and small, but here's a closer look at the two most prominent types of legend and lore.

CENTURIES

The brilliantly designed longships were swift, scary, majestic and versatile.

LONGSHIP

WHY THEY RATE Their sleek lines and unique warlike adornments signaled frightening raids among the European masses for 300 years.

DESIGN IN ACTION Longships were multioared marauders built for speed and purpose. They were long and slim and uniquely outfitted for swift seaworthiness over many nautical miles. Plus, a large, single square mast made out of wool and reinforced with double stitching helped the Vikings cut through the currents. Also, front and rear platforms were meant for hand-to-hand combat once the sea enemy was near enough to approach.

SIZE DID MATTER Types of longships were based on how many oar seats they had. The general purpose karv vessels might have 16 oar seats (eight on each side) and were used for fishing and hunting and, in some cases, warfare. You'd find

at least 20 rowing benches on the snekkja with a length of around 60 feet and a pretty small range from the hull top to the waterline. The skeid were larger warships (around 30 rowers) with a length up to 100 feet and a crew of 70. This was the largest among the type excavated in 1962 in Denmark, and dubbed the *Skuldelev 2*. Finally, the king of all longships—literally, since they were reserved for royalty—were the drakkar, or dragon ships. The pride of Scandinavia, these ships had the most ornate woodwork, the fiercest dragon face carvings at the front, and the longest lengths at around 160 feet. Throw in 34 oars per side and you have the kind of ship King Olaf Tryggvason of Norway led in 998 and dubbed *Long Serpent*.

POTENT PLUSES Between keel strength, sail maneuvering and size ratio, longships could reputedly achieve speeds of around 12 knots and travel about 125 miles in a day. The *Helge Ask*, a reconstructed version of a Skuldelev vessel, hit 15 knots. The low depth in waves meant it could ford a fjord or a stream, so getting in, striking fast and getting out played well to the Viking advantage.

MEMORABLE MINUSES If the wind currents weren't right, sailors could find themselves frequently using a wooden bailer to keep the water out of the ship. And with Vikings resting above board in two-man sleeping bags out in the open air, there wasn't much in the way of protection from the elements, unless the sail was lowered in a bad storm.

SKEID LONGSHIP

The modern clinker-built pilot gig boat owes its seaworthy strength to the longships of old.

VIKING SHIP DIY

So, you've done some basic woodworking—are you equal to the task of re-creating your own longship? Here's your 10-step guide to mimicking the skilled seafarers of yore. Warning: You'd better be plenty skilled for this challenge.

1 Split oak tree trunks into all the long, thin planks you'll need for hull and keel using your ax (the Vikings never used saws).

2 Lay out your sturdy keel in one or more sections of wood chocks.

3 Bolt boards with iron nails to your keel, and then to each other, each plank overlapping the next in what's called the clinker technique, creating resilience and flexibility.

4 Caulk it all to seal the overlap.

5 Continue adding the remainder of sideboards until you reach your desired height of freeboard.

6 Add internal supports to the hull and fasten a layer of floor planking to the boards using wooden pegs.

7 Bind the boards together with angled frame supports.

8 Add crossbeams (called stringers) to provide a deck and rowing benches.

9 Add your massive beam along the keel to support the mast.

10 Tie on the sail, add your oars and get ready to pillage (seats 20 to 60, depending on length of ship).

FIVE FOR FIGHTING

The Skuldelev discovery of five Viking ships offered an untold wealth of historical knowledge.

When the Gokstad longship was found and later unearthed from a frozen burial ground in Norway in 1880, it set the imagination reeling about Viking sea lore. But in many ways, it was the Skuldelev find that truly allowed Viking-philes to see the breadth of vessel development and splendor.

Five submerged ships were found in a shallow channel in Denmark's Roskilde fjord in 1962. Supposedly sunk in that spot to protect the entryway from enemy attack, the ships—now at the Viking Ship Museum in Roskilde—offer a fount of information about shipbuilding traditions and design. It was their variety that thrilled: Among the take was a stocky knarr with a 24-ton capacity and two majestic longships. And thanks to reproductions, 21st-century fans have been able to witness the range of what these ships were able to do. The discoveries included:

SKULDELEV 1 Stretching 52 feet long and 16 feet wide, this knarr, reputedly constructed of pine in western Norway in the early 11th century, may have navigated the North Atlantic Ocean and Baltic Sea. Approximately 60 percent of the ship was preserved as the Ottar.

SKULDELEV 2 This slender drakkar is said to have stretched some 92 feet long and about 15 feet wide, with 36 to 38 oarsmen on either side, who sat with only 2 feet 4 inches between them. The frames were broad enough to make the construction sturdy, and thin enough to create greater lightness.

SKULDELEV 3 Possibly another knarr (given its cargo hold), this Denmark-built oak ship would have been 45 feet by 15 feet and used for local sea travel. With room for a crew of up to six, *Skuldelev 3* was the kind of ship comfortable opening up the river systems of Russia and Constantinople.

SKULDELEV 4 Originally thought to be its own ship, this one was actually a different section of *Skuldelev 2*.

SKULDELEV 5 A swift-raiding warship measuring 60 feet long but only 8 feet wide, it would have had a lengthier range between its 24 rowers, allowing for longer strokes and darting attacks.

SKULDELEV 6 Measuring only 39 feet by 8 feet, this ship might have only been used for sailing (there's no evidence of oar ports). Perhaps it's a fishing vessel? Whatever it was, its presence adds yet more weight to Viking shipbuilding tactics and knowledge.

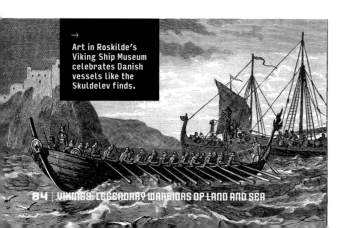

→ Art in Roskilde's Viking Ship Museum celebrates Danish vessels like the Skuldelev finds.

TRADE VESSEL

Cargo capacity was king on the mighty knarr that sailed the circular Norse trade routes.

KNARR

WHY THEY RATE Built for cargo and capacity, these booty-hauling vessels were welcome sights in trade cities throughout Scandinavia, Europe, Russia and the Middle East.

DESIGN IN ACTION Bulkier and stubbier than longships (standing around 50 feet in length), the knarr were sturdy enough to be stable in the swells, rode deeper in the water and could carry anything from livestock and settlers, to goods needed to keep farmers afloat during the cold weather months and tools for explorers to survey brave new worlds. While these ships had platforms fore and aft, the deep central hold area took up half the ship and allowed for the tonnage to be loaded aboard.

THAT MOST VERSATILE VESSEL Once the raiding was done, the knarr made far-flung trade routes possible. Drawing on designs modeled after the longship, the knarr's high, wide look made for much less bailing on the open seas. With a limited number of oars, the mast and sail were that much more important. And there would have been no trips to Greenland for Erik the Red without the knarr, which brought settlers in and oaken timber back to Greenland—so that more ships could be built.

POTENT PLUSES They were miracles of seaworthiness and carried at least 20 tons of goods.

MEMORABLE MINUSES The knarr were slower than the longships, and having potentially a wealth of goods on board and fewer seamen for protection made them more vulnerable to attack.

BUILDING A BETTER BOAT

1 DRAGON HEAD
The pièce de résistance of the Viking ships—these intricate bestial carvings protected the boats and their crew from adverse weather and the sea monsters of Norse mythology. More practically, the heads served as an intimidation tactic to frighten enemies.

2 HULL
Longship hulls were designed for speed using a shallow-draft design. The wide (up to 18 feet) hulls offered stability and balance, making the ship less likely to tip in strong winds.

3 KEEL
A keel was the first step to building a Viking ship. A piece of long, thin T- or V-shaped oak wood was selected and attached to the first hull planks.

4 OARPORT & OARS
Longships were fitted with oars that ran nearly the entire length of the boat. They were used when near a coast or river to propel without wind, and when a burst of speed was needed to get in or out of a location with ease. When not in use, oarports were sealed with wooden discs to keep the water out.

5 MAST & SAIL
While a longship sail has yet to be found intact, accounts depict them as square in shape, made of wool cloth and measuring approximately 35 to 40 feet across. In modern replicas, raising and lowering a Viking mast has been clocked in at just 90 seconds.

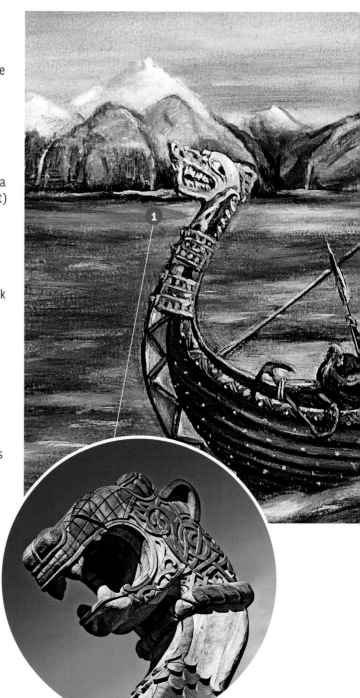

"Song of Canute" describes one of the Vikings' iconic ships: "His dragon with her sails of blue, all bright and brilliant to the view."

WHY BUY A BOAT....

When you can borrow one from a farmer? Surprisingly, many Viking boats were not owned by the kings, leaders or warriors themselves. In fact, they often didn't belong to the crown at all—instead, it was common practice for ships to be communally owned by coastal farmers and commissioned by the king when needed to quickly assemble a naval force.

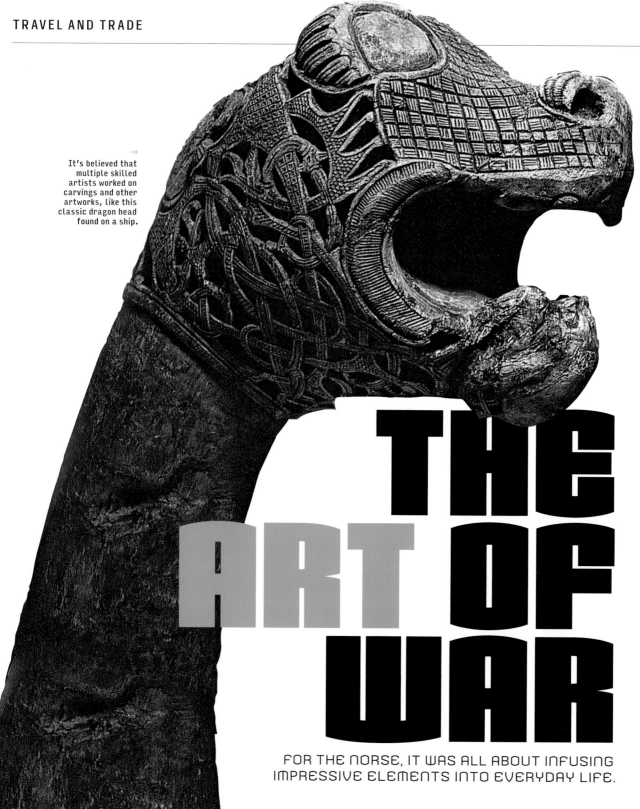

It's believed that multiple skilled artists worked on carvings and other artworks, like this classic dragon head found on a ship.

THE ART OF WAR

FOR THE NORSE, IT WAS ALL ABOUT INFUSING
IMPRESSIVE ELEMENTS INTO EVERYDAY LIFE.

Brooches, like this Borre-style fastener, were an integral part of a Viking woman's wardrobe.

The wooden carvings on the bow of a Viking ship showcase artistic craftsmanship.

In the years before the Renaissance, most Europeans lived in a society that valued function over fashion. But the Vikings thought, "Why not both?" Though nearly every item in Viking society had some practical use, the Norsemen's elaborate and intricate designs regularly adorned the humblest of items, from horseshoes to headposts.

Common Materials

As they favored carving and engraving techniques, the Vikings predominantly used wood, stone or metal for their creations. Though we can only really evaluate the items that have withstood the passage of time, it's thought that an assortment of less-common materials was once used as well. We catch glimpses of intricate designs in carved wood in well-preserved burial sites, particularly the Oseberg ship, which included a carved wooden cart, three sleighs and five 3D-carved animal

→
The Oseberg ship
was carefully
excavated,
offering us insight
into the art of the
ninth century.

headposts. In a rare case of artworks that didn't have a functional purpose, colorful wall tapestries made of leather or cloth have been found. Such luxury was generally reserved for those of exceedingly high status in the nomadic society.

Ornate Animals

Animals were present in nearly all Viking-era art, signifying important traits like power, strength and courage. Serpents, horses, birds, wolves and mythological creatures were regularly depicted, curved and intertwined to create ornate carvings.

Stylish Selections

Throughout the era, Viking art evolved and transformed into several distinguishable styles, each featuring abstract animals and loopy lines, but with its own take on the traditional look. Across the Viking-conquered world, different cultures influenced the artists, creating crossbred masterpieces. But for Scandinavians, the artwork of the era fell into one of six styles (or sometimes, a mix of them). These included:

STYLE E
LATE EIGHTH CENTURY TO LATE NINTH CENTURY
Most famously found on the Oseberg burial ship, this style is characterized by long, ribbon-shaped gripping animals with diminutive heads and wide eyes.

THE BORRE STYLE
MID–NINTH TO LATE 10TH CENTURY
Arguably the most popular and far-reaching of all the styles, the Borre featured beasts fitted with triangular heads and catlike features in interlaced, geometric designs.

THE JELLING STYLE
APPROXIMATELY 900 TO LATE 10TH CENTURY
Overlapping, and occasionally used in conjunction with the Borre style, the beasts on Jelling art are S-shaped and intertwined.

A rendering of Valhalla and Viking legend are engraved on this stone, found in Gotland, Sweden.

In classic Ringerike style, this tombstone from St. Paul's Cathedral depicts an abstract dragon carving.

"Virtually every item found from the Viking Age is highly decorated, even mundane, commonplace items."

WILLIAM R. SHORT IN
ICELANDERS IN THE VIKING AGE: THE PEOPLE OF THE SAGAS

→
This Urnes-style copper-alloy furnishing mount depicts a gaping-mouthed serpent.

→
A Mammen-style cross, depicting five interlaced dragons, was found in Braddan on the Isle of Man.

THE MAMMEN STYLE
APPROXIMATELY 950 TO 1000
Named after a carved ax head found in Mammen, Denmark, this style is a derivative of Jelling. Seminaturalistic birds and lions are featured alongside plant and foliate patterns.

THE RINGERIKE STYLE
LATE 10TH TO MID-11TH CENTURY
Similar to Mammen in the use of plants and beasts, the animals of Ringerike are long and curvy.

THE URNES STYLE
MID-11TH TO EARLY 12TH CENTURY
Named for the carved wooden panels of interlacing, serpentine animals found on the Stave church in Urnes, Norway, the animals of Urnes style feature long eyes pointed at the viewer.

Art for Art's Sake
A few centuries before the Renaissance would sweep Europe, when art would be embraced not as an afterthought but as a tool of its own meant to inspire and adore, the Vikings did their best to infuse beauty into their often-bloody world. Art for art's sake was rare, but it wouldn't be for long.

↓

"Animal motifs,
which have a
continuous tradition
in Scandinavia, are the
most important source for
stylistic classification."

*THE GROVE ENCYCLOPEDIA OF MEDIEVAL ART
AND ARCHITECTURE, VOLUME 1*

↑
This Jelling-style
disc brooch offers
a unique look at both
the artistry and the
jewelry of the day.

TRADERS

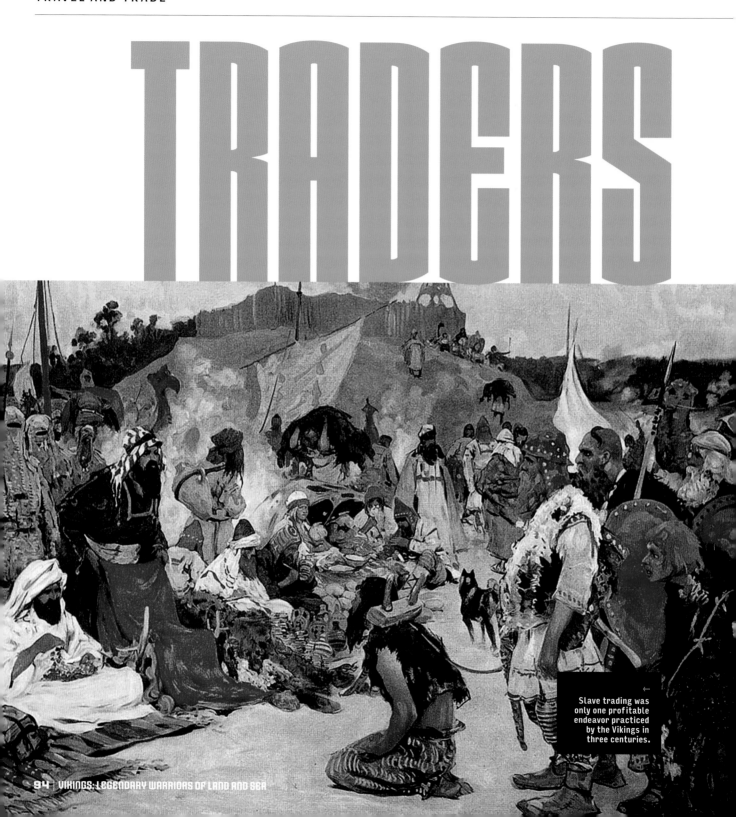

Slave trading was only one profitable endeavor practiced by the Vikings in three centuries.

MORE THAN RAIDERS

HISTORY IS SLOWLY REWRITING THE REPUTATION OF THE VIKINGS, WHO SPREAD WEALTH THROUGHOUT THE GLOBE.

Turn to the writings of the conquered Europeans who told the stirring, if tragic, Middle-Age tales, and the sagas that speak of brave Norse warriors who ran through their enemies, and you'll pretty much get the same picture: The Vikings were history's great horn-helmeted savages.

But what does it say about their skewed legacy that the misconception more popularly refuted is that the Vikings didn't wear horned helmets?

Every indication is that, at their worst, the Vikings practiced a cinematic savagery that would have made the *Game of Thrones* "red wedding" seem like just another day at the altar. But at their best, the Scandinavians had unquestionable impact as merchants, discoverers, hunters and sailors opening up trade routes. When it comes to shaping world history, Viking raiders will never hold a candle to Viking traders.

"They were extremely canny and obviously knowledgeable," says Lars Brownworth, author of *The Sea Wolves: A History of the Vikings*, among several books about the period. "And they built this incredible trading network, which stretched from the Middle East to Canada. It's extraordinary. Thugs don't do that."

Sport of Kings

In his book *The Age of the Vikings*, Anders Winroth, the Birgit Baldwin professor of history at Yale University, suggests it's impossible to overestimate the importance of Viking trade. "However disastrous and ruinous any individual Viking raid may have been for those attacked," he writes, "the overall impact of Scandinavian endeavors was, unexpectedly, to stimulate the economy of Western Europe. Trade and commerce had fallen to very low levels after the demise of the Roman Empire.... Europe was starved for gold and silver; European commerce needed an injection of precious metals, and the Vikings provided what was needed."

For the Vikings, trade was, in a phrase, a top-down economy. It began at the behest of the kings who understood that power was often a matter of show. The Danish King Godfrid had forged the town of Hedeby in the hopes of creating a trading mecca. His dream was more fully realized when he came up with a rather creative notion, and set off in 808 to sack the Slavic town of Reric on the Baltic Sea's southern shore. While he gave orders to destroy much, he advised to save all the merchants—and he simply carted them off and moved them closer to home in Hedeby. They set up shop once again, and Godfrid successfully boosted the local economy.

Getting in on the Action

Trade centers began to spring up in spots earmarked by royalty, chosen for their geographic advantages of being close to home, with good

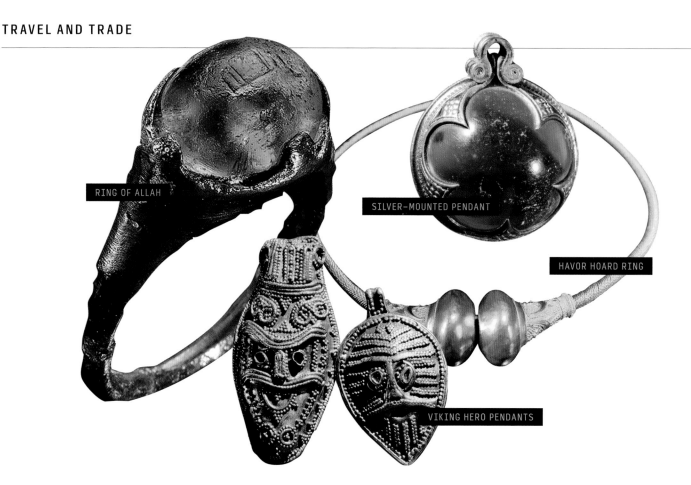

RING OF ALLAH

SILVER-MOUNTED PENDANT

HAVOR HOARD RING

VIKING HERO PENDANTS

proximity to the ports, easy enough overland access and with a setup that allowed for protection from interested plunderers. Much like the boomtowns that would one day populate the Wild West with each railroad stop being built, the trading posts became centers of activity and commerce welcomed by insiders, and great opportunities for outsiders.

For the majority of the people who have come to be called Vikings—meaning, the farmers, families and merchants who actually did more family raising than raiding—trade was a matter of practicality over plunder. Certain goods grown or hunted for were considered of great value in other parts of the world; meanwhile, some overseas goods could be counted on when the harshest of winters rolled in. Trading—interacting with other cultures, exchanging goods, practicing a kind

of local politics—made for its own excitement that you didn't have to risk your life for. And on a grander scale, it was the exchange of ideas, rumors, international gossip and other information that initially led the Vikings to understand the weakness of European capitals ripe for invading, and ultimately led them to see the greater advantages of accepting the culture and customs —not to mention faith—that made life easier. "Trade," Brownworth says, "is how they became aware of what was going on around them."

Art of the Barter

Early on, trade for the Viking populations was less about purchase through currency than it was about exchange through barter and bullion. In the years before Scandinavian kings minted their own coins, Arab coins were hot commodities, and most often were melted down for their silver, with the metal placed on the small but accurate weight scales that went into determining value. It was never, at that point, about numismatics so much as numbers: If you were short a little bit for your exchange, you might hack a coin in half to make up the difference. For reference, 8 ounces of silver could buy you four milk cows or 24 sheep.

The trade towns themselves thumped with a kind of excitement you'd normally associate with the likes of London. And while most of the sagas were sung about the raiders, it was really the traders and craftsmen whose talents helped to transform Scandinavia and usher it into a more modern age.

The locals came to market with their own goods: perishables, minerals from which tools and jewelry could be forged, rocks used to make whetstones or grindstones, and perhaps iron and soapstone. Pottery, jewelry, glass beads and the like were also on display. Farmers would show up with a generous length of sailcloth, woven together by village wives.

The Warmth of Wealth

The whalers, meanwhile, hunted in Norwegian seas, and found their own lucrative booty much prized elsewhere in the world. They reduced whale blubber to produce oil while also collecting the whalebone. Narwhal and walrus were hunted for skin and tusks, and horns were of particular value at the tables. Fur traders made a mint, as skins, tusks and hides were exchanged for silver and other goods that could be traded again, or luxury trinkets that symbolized one's own status. The furs were traded over long distances; given how cold the Scandinavian climes were, the warmth of those skins was in demand. Bird down, and reindeer and walrus skin (and reindeer antlers) fetched nice prices as well. Whale and sealskin, meanwhile, had

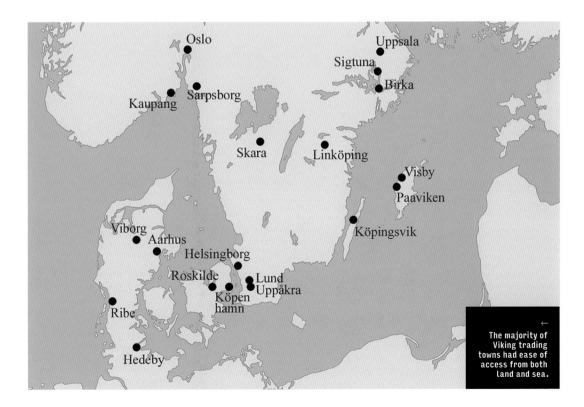

← The majority of Viking trading towns had ease of access from both land and sea.

their own uses to make ship cables on merchant and marauding vessels.

Slaves were among the most tradable commodities. In many cases, they came through commerce or capture in Russia, and were then sold through Europe; in other cases, prisoners taken in Western Europe would be sold in port cities in Scandinavia for around 12 ounces of silver each.

Ivory, honey, timber, amber, mercury, lead, jewelry, crystal, whalebone and hide ropes have been among the finds archaeologists have made in trading towns during the centuries since.

The traded goods brought into Scandinavia included items that were, again, considered either useful or prestigious. Salt and other spices or wine adorned the farmers' tables, while wool, glass and pottery poured in from Europe. Silk remained highly prized after coming in from Constantinople, the city once revered as the eastern capital of the Roman Empire. Kufic coins were highly sought-after imports from the Arab countries; over 85,000 such coins have since been found in Scandinavia, but they were treated as bullion on scales alongside French *deniers* and other foreign currency.

The Best Racket

The other coinage brought in came courtesy of "Danegeld," the racketeer-like ransom European kings paid to the plundering Norsemen for protection and the promise the Vikings would stop raiding. It was through those payments that Anglo-Saxon pennies found their way into the coffers of traders. Weapons were also among the more valued goods; the right kind of sword could fetch a considerable price on the market.

In all, trade as a tool proved invaluable, and continues to be, historically speaking. Thanks to tools and traded items excavated, archaeologists have been able to unearth a wealth of knowledge about Scandinavia and its strong links to the rest of the world in the time since.

"In Sweden, there was a hoard found and it had this jade Buddha from India, and you're clearly not raiding India. And I think that gives a better picture of the kind of trade network they built," says Brownworth of the Norse adventurers. "This was what the Vikings were doing during their 'day job.' I was at the Cloisters [museum last year in] Manhattan. And there's an ivory cross, carved by Irish monks made out of walrus ivory. But the walrus ivory is from North America. So, how does a monk in Ireland get hold of North American walrus ivory?" Brownworth thinks the answer is obvious: "It's from *trade*, with the Vikings. And there's just this little hint that there's a lot more going on here than we realize."

LEGEND HAS IT

As historian Anders Winroth reports in *The Age of the Vikings*, an Arab diplomat named Ibrahim ibn Yacoub al-Tartushi offered up a report based on a trip to the renowned trading port of Hedeby during the mid-10th century. Among his observations: "Inside [Hedeby] are many springs of sweet water. The inhabitants worship Sirius [they are pagan], except for a small number of Christians.... [The people] mostly eat fish" while many kill their newborns "to save the cost of raising them." And the truly awful singing he heard was "like the baying of hounds, only worse." This didn't exactly jibe with the impression of so vaunted a trade town but, like many such papers from that age, it could be subject to prejudices against the locals.

→ Metals forged by expert artisans fetched plenty of goods at barter trading tables.

99

"*Hedeby became an international town and the most important trading center in Scandinavia in the Viking Age.*"

KIRSTEN WOLF, IN *DAILY LIFE OF THE VIKINGS*

↑
Hedeby was both a thriving trade town and a bustling village for artists and business folk.

CITY OF GOLD

FOR A BRIEF TIME, HEDEBY WAS DENMARK'S
—AND THE WORLD'S—CROWN JEWEL OF COMMERCE.

Its main settlement was enclosed by a semicircle defense fortification extending some 4,265 feet heading north, west and south. To the east, an inlet with a sheltered harbor and wooden wharves invited the world. And the world came time and again to Hedeby, the Viking trading port with convenient entryway from England, the Frankish Kingdoms, Spain and beyond. Other trade towns such as Burka in Sweden and Kaupang in Norway bustled as well, but as writer Anders Winroth puts it in his book *The Age of the Vikings*, Hedeby became "the greatest Viking Age trade town of Scandinavia."

For more than 250 years, Hedeby was the city to exchange goods. Located near the Jutland Peninsula region that joins Denmark to northern Germany, Hedeby's streets were laid out in running right angles, with the fenced-in building lots used as homes or windowless

craftsman workshops. There, horn combs, glass beads, weavings, pottery, sword hilts and jewelry were forged for trade.

Its reputation made it valuable, but also controversial, and while the stalwart ramparts protected the city, it was only a matter of time before infighting got the better of it. In 1050, Norway's King Harald Hardrada, as part of his lengthy battle against Danish King Sweyn Estridsson, sent a number of burning ships into the harbor, destroying the place, and although some rebuilding occurred, a 1066 sacking destroyed it forever. Digs in the centuries since have uncovered some fascinating items, but it would be difficult to overstate the importance of the trading port that, about 1,000 years ago, helped run world commerce at, as one chronicler put it at the time, "the very end of the world's ocean."

X MARKS THE SPOT

UNEARTHED COINS AND OTHER RICHES REVEAL A LOT ABOUT THE VIKINGS.

→ With plunder from raids like the attack on the monastery at Lindisfarne, the Vikings had plenty of loot at their disposal.

103

One thousand years before Robert Louis Stevenson regaled the world with tales of buried loot, Vikings were building their own treasure islands—on Gotland, for one, a large island in the Baltic Sea where 700 silver hoards have been unearthed. Unfortunately for the original owners of these misplaced valuables, but luckily for modern-day archaeologists, many loot boxes were buried during troubled times, but were never recovered by their rightful owners. Gold, jewels, swords and coins have been found throughout the Viking world and trade routes. Sometimes the repository was, in essence, a savings account for a family to fall back on; sometimes it was more of a trophy case, but each one was undoubtedly hidden with a plan for reclamation.

Almost as quickly as one can hide treasure, there will be another person looking to dig it up, and so it goes for millennia. Today, however, historians, archaeologists and fortune seekers better understand and respect the valuable window into the culture and lifestyle that buried goods offer. The shiny objects that were once pocketed by eager hunters are now more often painstakingly preserved, documented and sent to museums to be studied and enjoyed.

Viking hoards don't just tell us about the day-to-day lives of Norse society, they also help us track the comings and goings of these nomadic people. Large deposits of Scandinavian artifacts have been excavated in far-off places like Canada and northwest Russia that would have required long voyages for Scandinavians to transport and then stash for safekeeping. These relics can often be time-stamped to within decades of their fabrication. Though most often found on islands, Viking stockpiles have been unearthed throughout Europe, Asia and the Americas—each telling their own story, each filled with their own veiled secrets of a long-gone era and each with a treasure hunter determined to dig up the past.

SEVEN HUMONGOUS FINDS
Hoen Hoard

Discovered near Buskerud, Norway, in 1834, it contained an array of dazzling, perfectly preserved jewelry. Often considered the most important Viking-era hoard ever found in Norway, the 207-piece stockpile included three gold arm rings, a gold brooch, 20 coins that had been made into pendants, 32 glass beads, two gold torcs (neck rings) and an additional 149 silver and gold objects. The find was exceptional not only for the amount of gold, but also because it offered unique insights into the jewelry of the day; today it can be seen at the Kulturhistorisk Museum in Oslo.

Vale of York Hoard

In 2007, near Harrogate, England, 617 coins and 65 silver objects were found undisturbed in an elegant, gold-lined vessel. The coins hail from across the Vikings' known world and give us a unique look at their voyages: They were minted in such far-flung places as England, Ireland, Sweden, Russia, France, Baghdad and North Africa. Even more interesting: Some contain a mix of Christian and pagan imagery, revealing a bit about the beliefs of the newly converted Vikings. The ornate container (sometimes identified as a cup or bowl) was traced to ninth-century northern

France, and may have been pillaged or received as a gift. Intricate designs decorate the vessel, including running animals, leaves and vines. "Treasure cases are always interesting, but this is one of the most exciting cases that I have ever had to rule on," North Yorkshire coroner Geoff Fell said at the time. The collection was likely buried upon the expulsion of the Vikings from York in the 10th century.

Arlanda Airport Hoard

It seems that the site of the Arlanda International Airport in Stockholm has always attracted travelers and adventurers alike. The trove, excavated from the area in 2008, yielded a huge number of Arabic coins. Minted between 800 and 840 and hailing from across the Arabic peninsula and Western Asia, the find was especially unique because of its placement: While the vast majority of loot has been discovered on Sweden's islands, the Arlanda Airport cache was deposited on the mainland.

Cuerdale Hoard

Providing us with an encyclopedia-like sampling of Viking artifacts, the Cuerdale cache is notable both for its size and the variety of its treasures. Found in England in 1840 during repair work to the bank of the River Ribble, the 8,600 pieces are not your average coin collection: They also include torcs, ingots, brooches and chains and other items. Recovered intact in a lead box, the complete set was turned over to Queen Victoria—minus a coin for each workman involved in the discovery. Many of the pieces can now be seen in the British Museum in London.

Spillings Hoard

The island of Gotland is the gift that keeps on giving in the treasure hunter world. In 1999, an unheard-of 14,295 coins (nearly all Islamic in origin) were excavated in the largest-known Viking stockpile found to date. The impressive collection of silver weighed in at nearly 150 pounds, and contained 486 silver arm rings, among other

> **Most hoards were discovered "by accident during road building in the 19th century or just hauled out of the ground" by amateur diggers.**
>
> VIKING SPECIALIST
> OLWYN OWEN

items. It's believed the loot was buried beneath the floorboards of a ninth-century Viking outhouse.

Because Gotland is practically overflowing with Viking treasure (180,000 coins have been found there, in comparison to mainland Sweden, where just 80,000 have been unearthed), metal detecting is now banned without prior approval for a scientific survey.

The Galloway Hoard

When British metal detectorist Derek McLennan came upon an arm ring 2 feet underground in a Dumfries and Galloway field in Scotland back in 2014, he couldn't have possibly guessed he was about to unearth the most extensive Viking trove in U.K. history. Immediately recognizing the significance of his find, McLennan contacted the Scottish Treasure Trove Unit, which swiftly sent an archaeologist to expertly excavate the area. A 10th-century vessel was dug up, filled to the brim with silver bracelets and brooches, gold jewelry, including a bird-shaped pin and a ring, a Christian cross and a variety of other artifacts. "It's a strange and wonderful selection of objects," Olwyn Owen, a scholar and Viking specialist in Edinburgh, said of the discovery when it was found. In thanks for finding the bounty and in exchange for handing over the loot, McLennan was awarded £2 million (its market value), or about $2.5 million today.

The Rügen Hoard

A unique cache was located by two amateur archaeologists on the German island of Rügen in the Baltic Sea. A 13-year-old boy and his metal-detecting partner first spotted a single silver coin in a field near the village of Schaprode, but when the state archaeology office got involved, they realized the magnitude of the find. Hundreds of silver coins, likely dating to the 10th-century reign of King Harald "Bluetooth" Gormsson, were uncovered, along with a piece of jewelry depicting Thor's famous hammer. Archaeologists called the hoard the "biggest trove of such coins in the southeastern Baltic Region."

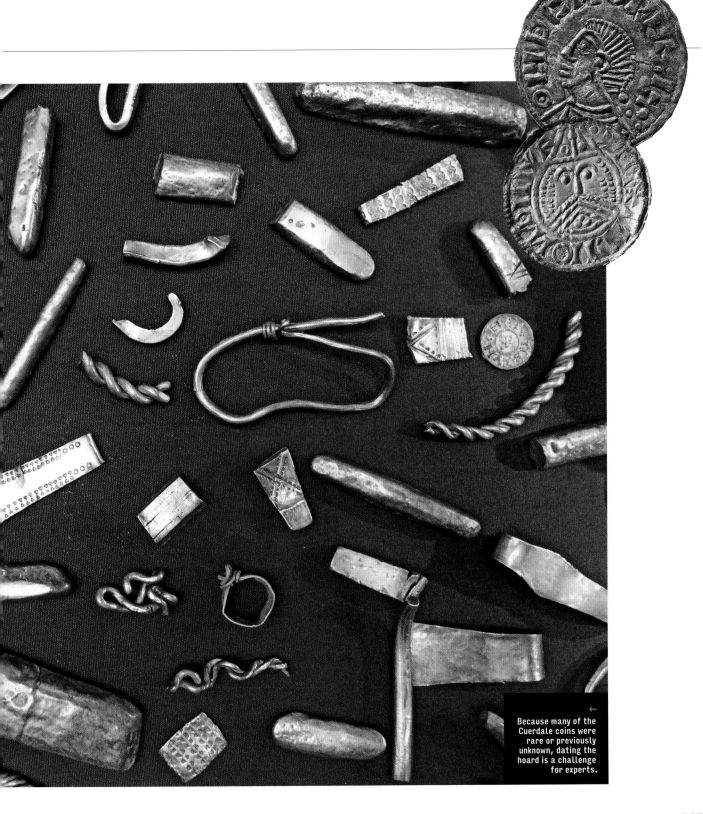

Because many of the Cuerdale coins were rare or previously unknown, dating the hoard is a challenge for experts.

A WHOLE NEW WORLD

LEIF ERIKSON CHANGED HISTORY BY COLONIZING NORTH AMERICA FIRST, EVEN THOUGH THE EFFORT WOULDN'T LAST.

→ Leif, immortalized in a statue

They'd heard all the tales. It was a coast rich in resources. One glance at the shoreline and you could see a gentle slope feeding upward, all covered with vast troves of trees. Everything about the land was kind, the stories said; not at all like the harshness of Greenland. And the images filled Leif Erikson's mind with wonder.

That's how it began: the quest, some 1,000 years ago, to settle in the Americas. In the 500-some-odd years before Columbus sailed from Spain, North America—specifically, Newfoundland and parts of Canada—became a setting for sagas, and a stopgap place for the Vikings to perhaps save their colonization of the land Leif's father, Erik the Red, had come to call home. It was the first time the New World truly inspired the European imagination; clearly, it wouldn't be the last.

Erik had named his own discovered island "Greenland" in part as a ploy to bring more settlers to its difficult clime. Though he owned the best tracts of land, it didn't stop others from following his lead and farming in the more temperate areas. The sea provided plenty of meat, and even sealskin and walrus ivory for use and trade. But timber was scarce beyond the driftwood, making the majority of the land not nearly inhabitable enough.

And there were also those tales of a land of warmth and plenty, and the itch to rediscover them. The stories had been spun by Bjarni Herjólfsson, a trader who'd gone to visit his father in Greenland and found himself, along his extended journey, stumbling upon a place farther west, with timberland so limitless the Vikings came to name it Tree Land, or in their words, Markland.

A Journey Begins

Some 15 years later, Leif decided he wanted to see this vaunted place for himself. Bjarni, now the wealthy inheritor of his father's estate, had no interest, but his onetime crew—and their ship—was at the ready for Leif, and the sailors remembered the way. Leif wanted his father, Erik, to lead the adventure, and while the sagas differ on why he chose not to (did he really fall off his horse

on the way to the longship, taking it as a bad sign and declaring that he wasn't destined to discover any other lands?), Leif ended up being master of his own destiny. And off they sailed.

Following Bjarni's route backward toward their destination, it didn't take very long, and the crew of 35 first came upon a land with tall black glaciers, which they named Hulluland (what is now known as the Baffin Islands).

In due course, they came next to the land of opportunity so described by Bjarni, which the crew immediately recognized. It more than lived up to its name. It was, as historians have described it, a "well-wooded country, where pine trees fit for masts grew in great abundance. Long, low beaches covered with white, glistening sand stretched as far as the eye could reach; and, inland, lost themselves in flat plains on which the forests grew."

Let the Wine Flow

They passed Markland, now the Labrador half of the Newfoundland and Labrador Canadian province, and sailed four more days to another beautiful part of the world, and continued until they found a hospitable shore south of the island they'd been sailing past. Crossing the sand with their hammocks, Leif and his crew saw equally rich forests and grazing grass. Inland salmon—large and plentiful—swam through the rivers. It looked like paradise.

Leif decided to stay for the winter, which felt a great deal milder than Greenland's, and with daylight lasting longer. In a panic one day after noticing the disappearance of Tyrker, the man he considered his foster father, Leif organized a search party, only to find the man smiling and suddenly among them with two new discoveries: wild wheat, and perhaps more importantly, grapes suitable for fermenting. The wine they produced made the trip that much more merry, and inspired Leif's naming of the place: Vinland. Like his dad, Leif thought an enticing name would bring more settlers over, although his guess was that they'd need little motivation, given the setting.

When summer came, the crew returned to Greenland packed to the gills with berries and timber, and a promise for more. But when his famed father died of a plague soon after Leif's return, the son was obliged to remain and—like Bjarni before him—leave the exploring and colonizing to others.

Turned Tables

While the tale of America's discovery is a romantic one, it wasn't destined to continue with a similar theme. It turned out the Vikings were meant to find—much as Columbus one day would—that their "New World" was already someone else's Old World.

Leif's younger brother Thorvald was the first European to make direct contact with the Native peoples living in that part of America, who were perhaps either the Inuit Eskimos or Algonquin Indians. After a winter spent at Leif's settlement—during which time they feasted on salmon and a confusingly smaller grouping of berries—they sailed farther south and made shore on a coast that had three canoes in the distance... each with strangers hiding beneath. The Vikings gave chase and killed all but one, who escaped. Upon further inspection, they noticed a small village over a nearby hill.

In short time, the Natives—whom they called "Skræling," an insulting term related to the unfamiliar screeching sounds they made—returned for battle, with only Thorvald himself being injured by arrow fire that would soon cost him his life. Understandably dejected, the crew quickly left for their Greenland home.

Other expeditions returned to the new country, perhaps the most noted (in the sagas) being the one headed by Leif's brother-in-law, Thorfinn Karlsefni, with, famously, Leif's controversial sister Freydís aboard. At first, the colonists found themselves somewhat welcome by the Native populations; they settled well and, as usual, engaged in profitable trading. But in time, the Natives attacked. The reason remains a mystery. Was one Native killed after attempting to trade

→
Leif took his men on a historic, world-building journey.

"Leif...lighted upon lands of which before he had no expectation. There were wheat fields and the vine-tree in full growth."

FROM *THE SAGA OF ERIK THE RED*

↓
Reconstructed houses in Newfoundland give a look at how Leif and his followers lived.

LEGEND HAS IT

Two separate sagas tell the tale of Leif's journey: *The Saga of the Greenlanders* and *The Saga of Erik the Red*. The former indicates that Bjarni Herjólfsson first laid eyes on the New World, stumbling upon it during his attempt to visit his father. But amazingly—if not surprisingly, given the strange disparities in these sagas—*The Saga of Erik the Red* gives no mention at all of Bjarni, with Leif getting all the glory as discoverer of the lands. It also suggests Leif was the one who stumbled upon the New World after leaving Norway with instructions from King Olaf Tryggvason to baptize all the Greenlanders as Christians.

for Viking weapons? Or did the Indians begin to suspect evil intentions among the settlers? Either way, a battle began, and while the sagas give much credit to Freydís for helping to disburse the marauders, other attacks quickly followed. With winters also growing more inhospitable, a return to Greenland was inevitable. Expeditions would occasionally return for timber but given the strife with the Natives, the idea of fully colonizing the New World had come to an end. As the sagas put it, "It seems plain that though the quality of the land was admirable, there would always be fear and strife dogging them on account of those who already inhabited the land."

The move would also, by extension, spell the end of the Viking settlement in Greenland; without the influx of this new source of timber, there would be no way to sustain it.

But Leif's dream had been realized, and the literature written about the journey, read in time by Columbus, continued to inspire. Had the Vikings been more determined, there's no way to predict how history might have shifted as a result.

"It's one of these historical 'what-ifs,'" says Lars Brownworth, author of *The Sea Wolves: A History of the Vikings*. "Had the North American experiment worked, obviously there's more resources than they could use in Greenland. It would have been a much different world."

ANGELS OF DEATH

THOUGH KNOWN FOR THEIR MERCILESS, MURDEROUS TENDENCIES, VIKINGS PLACED MUCH CARE IN PLANNING THE FINAL FAREWELLS OF FRIENDS AND FAMILY.

The After

Influenced greatly by their pagan religion, the Vikings and their burial rituals are well-understood due to the significant number of archaeological artifacts, which are often not so different from today's. A Viking's death, the Norse believed, would lead to an afterlife in one of the nine realms. Among them were Valhalla (The Hall of the Fallen) and Fólkvangr (The Field of the People), ruled by Odin and Freyja, respectively,

In the hopes of entering Valhalla, men were laid to rest alongside their weapons and warrior wares—their use would be just as important in their next life of battle.

↑
North of Aalborg, Denmark, the largest burial site in Scandinavia has graves dating back to Viking times.

→ For a burial by boat, the body of the deceased and all he would need in his next life were packed up and pushed out to sea.

← This tent-like wooden burial chamber is from the deck of the Oseberg ship.

both resting places for fallen warriors. Odin and his Valkyries chose worthy warriors for Valhalla, who would fight and feast alongside the gods, preparing for the final battle of Ragnarök. Fifty percent of warriors made their way to Fólkvangr, though a lack of sources make details on the conditions there sparse. There was also Helheim, an undesirable underworld overseen by the goddess Hel. Helheim was reserved for those who died a "dishonorable" death—by Viking standards, that is—such as old age or disease. And finally there was Helgafjell, where the souls of the Norse who were not warriors, but who, it was assumed, had led exceptionally good lives to reap such a reward. They would spend their eternity enjoying

the best of life, drinking and socializing on the holy mountain. Occasionally, those who died at sea were taken to the underwater home of the giantess Rán, who personified the sinister side of the sea and ruled the realm of the dead.

The promise of an afterlife informed many steps in the burial and funeral process, as the Norsemen worked to ensure their loved ones would end up in the correct resting place. Funeral goods and gifts were carefully matched to the deceased, be they men or women. If the send-off did not properly match the social group, a Viking's soul could end up lost, wandering eternally with no final destination in which to settle.

Bountiful Burials

Like today, there were several customary types of burials to choose from—cremation, a traditional burial and, yes, burial at sea, though the latter is much less common than popular culture might have you believe. Traditions varied greatly throughout Viking society, and it's estimated that something like 50 percent of people were never interred in a formal grave, due to low social status, poverty or slavery. The most common Viking farewell was cremation followed by placement in a grave or under a pile of rocks, which allowed the smoke to carry the Viking soul swiftly to the afterlife.

Without access to today's cremation chambers— which reach between 1,400 and 1,800 degrees Fahrenheit—a funeral pyre was required to effectively break down the bones of a human body. To build a pyre, the body was placed strategically across a large pile of wood, and left for many hours to ensure the fire would burn the body correctly.

Many Viking graveyards have been discovered throughout Europe. Sometimes, groups were buried under grave mounds, which were often built to resemble ships using stones to outline the shape of the boat. The incorporation of a vessel was common, symbolizing a safe passage to the afterlife.

Still, the best-known (yet least-used) form of burial was that at sea. A ship was a valuable

The open-air pyre allowed the wind to carry the soul off to Valhalla.

↑
Funeral goods tell us about the Vikings, from what they wore to whom they traded with.

commodity in Viking society, and since a burial at sea was reserved only for those of a high social status—sea captains, the ultra wealthy and noble warriors—those sent out were usually accompanied by their funeral goods and grave offerings. While commonly depicted as a burning ship cast off, in practice, the body was generally cremated and then placed on the ship. One of the most famous boat funerals known today was that of the Oseberg ship, a burial of two women, one who was between 70 and 80 years of age, the other a little over 50, who died around 834. Because the ship was found largely intact in Norway in 1904 (over 90 percent of the original timber remained), archaeologists were able to glean extensive insight into what it meant to be buried at sea. The ship ran 70 feet long by 17 feet wide and could fit up to 30 people, and the women were buried with a considerable fortune in gifts and jewels. The burial was, quite literally, fit for a queen (or two!).

The Darker Side of Death

While many of the Viking's customs are familiar to modern-day people, others reflect the more barbaric aspects of their society. It was not uncommon for horses, slaves and sometimes wives to be offered as grave goods; the women could then be raped by villagers, and ultimately killed and buried alongside the deceased as a sign of reverence and of their power. In at least one instance, the 10th-century Arab Muslim writer Ahmad ibn Fadlan described a funeral he witnessed on a Viking trade route, crediting an old woman—whom he dubbed the Angel of Death—as the guide of these cruel proceedings.

A Rowdy Reception

Today's raucous Irish funerals may take a page from the requiems of their former conquerors. The Vikings would wait for seven days before the celebration, and on the seventh day would mark the passing by drinking copious amounts of ale. This moment also signified the official passing of any property from the deceased to his or her heirs, who would receive their inheritance. Again, according to ibn Fadlan, a poor man passed with little pomp and circumstance, but for a noble man, a third of his wealth would go to his family, a third to pay for funeral clothes, and a third to the alcoholic drink *nabidh*, to be imbibed at the man's cremation. Several runestones also chronicle the process of inheritance. The Hillersjö stone tells of

a woman who received the property of her children and grandchildren, an example of a woman's right to inheritance that was first chronicled in Scandinavia in the fifth century.

The End

And so, for the Vikings, burial traditions were a combination of good and evil, not unlike the stories of the gods they so revered. The traditions tell us much of their societal hierarchy and gender roles. Wealthy women could receive a dignified burial and inheritance, but slave girls could be raped and murdered in sacrifice. Still, for most freemen, the utmost care was taken in preparing for the afterlife, as friends and family worked tirelessly to ensure the souls of their loved ones would live on eternally. Perhaps, if the lore is to be believed, 1,000 years later, the lost souls continue to drift, while the fallen Vikings of Valhalla continue to prepare for their final battle.

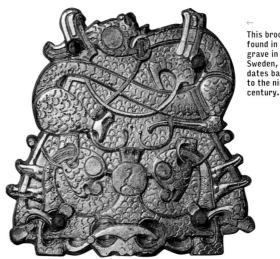

← This brooch, found in a grave in Sweden, dates back to the ninth century.

CHAPTER 4

A CULTURE THAT THRIVED

THEY WEREN'T JUST FEARSOME FIGHTERS:
BACK ON THE HOME FRONT, FAMILY AND FARMING
TOOK PRIORITY, ALONG WITH SOME FUN AND GAMES.

A DAY IN THE LIFE

SEAFARING? BUT THERE'S FARMING TO BE DONE!

The daily life of a Viking wasn't all navigating the high seas and conquering new lands. There was a life to be maintained on the home front, even for warriors.

Shaping Societal Order

After capturing slaves on their seafaring voyages, Vikings regularly brought them back to Scandinavia, where they'd join the lowest class in Viking society: the thralls. Made up of slaves born or captured and citizens who'd gone bankrupt, life was not pleasant for those lowest on the totem pole: Archaeologists have found slave collars and regular proof of sacrifices—thralls sent out to sea to sail into eternity with their masters.

Next up in the social order: the freemen (or *karlar*), who made up the middle class. These were the Viking warriors. They were also farmers or craftsmen, often trading in their shovels for swords when an expedition arose.

And then there were the earls—the chieftains and warrior leaders who had amassed great wealth and power through battle. Second only to kings, the earls were looked upon as aristocrats, taking over royal and leadership duties in the new lands.

FURS AND JEWELS

FEMALE GARB

RUNESTONE

VIKING BOOT

> "Small pieces of bone and antler were shaped into finger rings, gaming pieces or amulets..."
>
> JORVIK VIKING CENTRE

A Viking settlement at Jarlshof on the Shetland Islands.

FRAME HOUSE

BARRACKS

A Static Job Market

Vikings were, by and large, farmers by trade, and their time off the water revolved around subsistence farming—from planting to fertilizing to picking the crops each season. Harvest took an all-hands-on-deck approach, with women and children joining in to complete the task before the first winter frost.

For a man or a single woman in early Viking society, a jack-of-all-trades approach was important to daily life. A farmer was also a carpenter, a veterinarian and a herdsman, as he or she single-handedly worked to keep the homestead afloat.

As the years went on and the societies grew more sophisticated, organized markets began to pop up in village centers. Specialized craftspeople like blacksmiths, jewelers, potters and leatherworkers grew in popularity alongside warriors, sailors, hunters and farmers. Together, they would sell and trade their wares and skill sets.

The life of a Viking-era farmer may seem romantically simple, but in truth, the work was grueling. And between the famine and disease they faced, 30 to 40 percent of children died before ever reaching adulthood.

Meals for Families

For the Dark Ages, the Vikings dined on a decent diet. Protein-heavy food including pork, reindeer, elk, lamb and goat was often plentiful for peasants and royals alike. Fresh fruit and veggies like cabbage, carrots and apples, plus locally sourced and traded spices, helped to kick mealtime up a notch.

In the morning, a family would eat the *dagmal* (day meal), typically an hour after waking up, consisting of the previous evening's leftovers: bread and fruit for adults, and porridge, milk and bread for children. In the evening, a fish or meat was cooked over a hearth with vegetables, often in a stew. Dessert was limited to honey, the sole sweetener in their society.

Local celebrations centered around a feast, generally hosted at the home of a king or local chief. The delicious spread was complemented with good company and served as a bonding social experience for the locals at all levels of society.

Costumes and Clothing

Experts continue to debate the ins and outs of Viking fashion, as very few garments survived the centuries intact. Instead, we have many examples of fabric (usually wool, linen and animal skin) and color (red was especially expensive and exotic, because the madder root plant, used for dye, could not be found in Scandinavia).

Standard garb for men included layers of shirts and pants to withstand the frigid Nordic temperatures. For women, it was ankle-length woolen dresses with linen under-dresses beneath them. With a rainbow of colors and patterns to choose from, and many capable seamstresses, the clothing is thought to have been quite bright and cheerful, a contrast to the bitter, bleary days the people often faced.

Sheltering From Storms

For most Viking families, longhouses consisted of a single large room, where humans and animals alike sheltered and rested. Occasionally, the single room was split into two, allowing men to separate their sleeping quarters from that of their furry friends. As the wealth of some Vikings grew, their longhouses got longer. These Norse McMansions—up to 250 feet long—often boasted separate quarters for food preparation, livestock and living areas.

Travel by Ice

When they weren't out on the open seas, Vikings mostly traveled by boat, horse, cart and wagons. But in frozen Scandinavia, the Northerners had to get a little creative: Archaeologists have found more than 100 pinewood skis that Vikings would use to travel over icy terrain. Horses were also fitted with spiked footwear on their hooves to cross icy waters!

Between long days at the office and feasts with their friends and neighbors, for most Viking families, life had its challenges. But in many ways, it wasn't so different than today.

→
In Norse mythology, a Valkyrie decides who may live and who may die in battle.

VIKING QUEENS

DISCOVER THE SECRETS OF THE
LOST LADIES OF NORSE SOCIETY.

In the mind's eye, the word Viking inevitably conjures up the traditional image of a bearded brute, a fierce warrior and, always, a man. But in a society built upon exploration and resettlement, women played a vital role in the success of the Viking Age as the keepers of the home front—wherever that home turned out to be. From queens to peasants, female Vikings had a variety of social statuses and were, perhaps surprisingly, even able to enjoy lives as businesswomen and traders in the event of their husband's death.

They could own property and legally divorce, but were subject to prearranged marriages. A woman could collect an inheritance, but could not appear in court or hold any political power. The highs and lows of a female in Viking society were invariably better than those of many other women of the time, but in comparison to their male counterparts, who have runes, sagas and songs devoted to their stories, our understanding of the female Viking is pieced together largely by studying grave sites and burials.

Early Equality

If there was ever a doubt that women could achieve the highest levels of Viking society, one needs to look no further than the most elaborate, lavish burial site ever discovered from the Viking Age: the Oseberg ship. The two women buried within the ship's walls had, quite clearly, achieved the pinnacle of status in Viking society. After a short investigation of the ship, it was immediately apparent to experts that this burial was fit for a literal queen: The boat was packed with all of the amenities the women could have ever needed on their journey to the underworld, from enough food for a feast, to looms for keeping busy, to bedding for comfortable sleep.

Heart of the Home

Life for the typical Viking woman could be summed up swiftly by looking at another burial site, that of a woman found in Norway in the 1960s who lived 1,000 years ago. She was laid

> ## "Archaeological evidence... of burials shows that Scandinavian women (identified largely by their jewelry) reached places as far apart as Greenland and Russia."
>
> FROM *WOMEN IN THE VIKING AGE* BY JUDITH JESCH

to rest in a typical ninth-century Norse burial, surrounded by the tools that helped her most in life: a pair of wool combs, a weaving batten, a bronze basin, a knife and a pair of shears, all illustrating her ties to the domestic home. There was a sickle to represent her outdoor work, as well as jewelry made of glass, silver and gold. Even more telling, she was buried with her infant child in her arms and loot—including an Anglo-Saxon pendant, likely given to her by her warrior husband after he plundered an English town.

This unnamed ninth-century woman represents the majority of the women of her time: a housewife consumed with home and family. While their

NORSE HOUSE

husbands went to war, women managed the housekeeping, cooking, children and farm, laboring to ensure a bountiful harvest that the family would count on for sustenance in the winter months ahead. Women were also responsible for weaving and sewing, and bearing and raising the children. The lack of women warriors was likely at least in part because their plates were already full.

Female Freedoms

The majority of unearthed Viking burial sites certainly reflect these traditional gender roles: Men were buried with their weapons and tools; women with household items, needlework and jewelry. Yet women in the Viking era enjoyed a decent amount of freedom for their day. Notably, they could legally separate from their husband if he did not return from his travels after three years or if the family was thrust into poverty. Perhaps most notably for a woman's rights, if her husband or his family was violent toward her, striking her more than three times, a divorce could be granted. The writings of those from other lands illuminate how unusual the freedoms Viking women enjoyed were: Spanish-Arabic author At-Tartushi noted he was surprised by a woman's right to divorce in the 900s.

Warrior Women

Records remain scarce when it comes to women engaging in warfare. The hopes for a real-life female Valkyrie seem unsound—although sorceresses, who would use magic to influence a battle's outcome, were plentiful. Still, Danish historian Saxo Grammaticus wrote in the 12th century of "shield-maidens" who dressed in men's uniforms and practiced sword-fighting and knife-wielding. Few accounts of these shield-maidens taking to battle can be found or verified. Grammaticus once wrote of one such woman—called Lagertha—fighting alongside famed Viking Ragnar Lothbrok; he fell in love with her fortitude

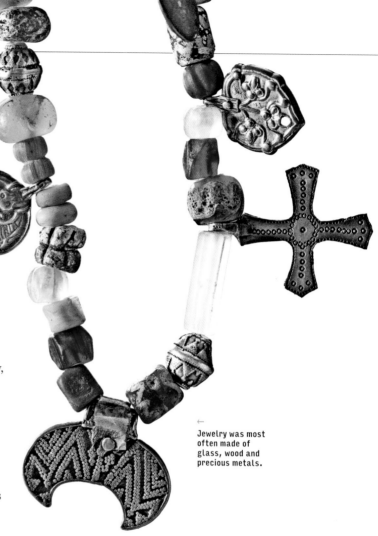

Jewelry was most often made of glass, wood and precious metals.

and asked for her hand in marriage. This story, however engaging, remains relegated to myth, not history. Still, the fable shows that a Viking woman's drive was not to be looked down upon or snuffed out, but to be admired and respected.

Unfortunately, the life of a housewife is usually relegated to the ash heaps of history, and as such the image of Viking women is unlikely to change. But when we take a closer look, these warrior women—whether they "fought" on the farm or on the battlefield—affected every aspect of Viking society, and ultimately changed the future of the world.

Described in the "Saga of King Olaf," King Canute and Ulf the Earl play what is considered the earliest recorded game of chess in the Norse lands.

→
Vikings would propose a toast by raising their drinking horns and saying "skål" ("cheers!").

SPORTS & GAMES

FOR VIKINGS ON THE HOME FRONT, LEISURE WAS A SPORT ALL ITS OWN.

When Vikings weren't busy on the battlefield, games of sport, strength and strategy were popular pastimes in this era. A work-hard, play-hard approach to life led to the creation of everything from board games to ballgames to make-believe games.

Buried Board Games

Mentioned in the mythological poem "Völuspá," board games were held in high enough regard to be played by the gods. After the demise of the gods in the tale, the reappearance of golden playing pieces is cited as a sign of good luck.

> "Alcohol played an important role in Viking political life, bringing men together in an atmosphere of peaceful solidarity."
>
> CHARLES RISELEY ON "CEREMONIAL DRINKING IN THE VIKING AGE"

After the feast, Vikings often continued to play games all through the night.

LOKI BEI AEGIRS GASTMA

Because games pieces are commonly found among grave goods, historians have cobbled together the outlines of many of the popular games of the time. Boards ranging from 7x7 squares to 19x19 squares, pieces made of bone and wood, and loaded dice have all been found.

A modified form of chess was enjoyed, and while gambling was outlawed in Iceland, strategic skill was revered—as King Eysteinn and King Sigurðr show in the Old Norse saga *Morkinskinna*, in which Eysteinn admits to his subpar swimming ability but counters, "I am more skilled and better at board games, and that is worth as much as your strength."

Feasts of Fun

Imbibing alcohol to excess wasn't just accepted in Viking culture; it was often encouraged, and gave way to the creation of many mead-friendly games. At feasts and celebrations, guests were assigned partners and the pair would drink together throughout the evening. The higher-ranking men were matched with a woman, but as the male-female ratio dwindled, men were often paired with each other.

Verbal sparring led to *flyting*, somewhat akin to a Viking rap battle. Participants in this game traded verses of poetry, boasting of their own strength while ridiculing their opponent. Imagine: a Comedy Central roast with a warrior vibe.

Once the feast ended, a game of *hnútukast*, a primitive, dangerous version of dodgeball, would often commence. Using the leftover bones from the meal, players would target each other, intending to maximize injury with each projectile thrown. The high-stakes game had serious side effects—in the tale *Hrólfs Saga Kraka*, it's revealed that one man was killed after taking a bone to the head.

Play Ball!

Though the first modern Olympics were still 1,000 years away, the sagas are packed with stories of sport. Competitions in swimming, wrestling, horse fighting and ballgames all made appearances; the

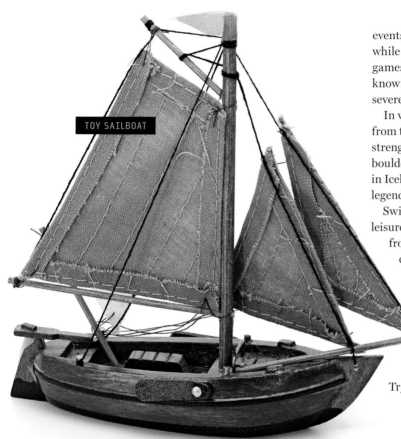

TOY SAILBOAT

events were designed to strengthen social bonds while also honing battle skills. These aggressive games were generally male-dominated and were known to get highly combative, often leading to severe injury or death.

In weightlifting competitions not so different from today's, participants competed in a match of strength—the participant who lifted the largest boulder was crowned the winner. Today, boulders in Iceland attest to the historical tales of the legendary strongmen of the sagas.

Swimming was popular for both sport and leisure, though competitions looked quite different from a Michael Phelps-esque race: In many cases, Vikings entered a swim competition with the goal of drowning the opponent, and at times competed with their armor on.

Tests of strength, agility and endurance were often enjoyed, including tugs-of-war and rock climbing. Then there was King Olaf Tryggvason of Norway, who was famously said to walk from one end of his ship to the other on the oars of his sailors as they rowed on.

Child's Play

No matter the year on the calendar, children will always want to play, and Viking tykes were no exception. Though considered grown by age 12, and often working long days well before approaching puberty, young children still enjoyed similar wooden toys to those seen today, including miniature weapons, felt balls and items carved to look like ships and horses.

Living in a society where life was uncertain, people were always on the move, and death and destruction were constants, sports and games were a source of great pleasure for children and adults alike. While little importance was given to formal education, the focus instead was on training for the brutal wars Vikings often found themselves engaged in, including learning about swords, shields, spears, stone-throwing and bow-and-arrow shooting—all essential skills necessary to help prepare for the battlefield.

"The sport of swimming consisted of two competitors wrestling each other underwater to prevent the other one from surfacing and catching his breath."

FROM *FOX TOSSING: AND OTHER FORGOTTEN AND DANGEROUS SPORTS, PASTIMES, AND GAMES* BY EDWARD BROOKE-HITCHING

A BOARD GAME

↑
Popular strategy board games similar to chess were played on a checkered or latticed game board.

LAW AND ORDER

FORGET BATTLES AND BLOODSHED:
VIKINGS WANTED THEIR DAY IN COURT.

While the Vikings were no strangers to fighting on foreign battlefields, there were just as many at-home altercations that required mediation—and these conflicts generally couldn't be solved with swords and shields.

What the Vikings lacked in tact, they made up for in honor. At the core of most every Norseman's value system was a belief in fairness and justice that was anchored by the stories of the righteous gods. This created a society ripe for a robust legal system built around the tenets of law and order. Still, in early Viking times, a lack of a societal center made this a daunting task—that is, until the introduction of the Thing.

The Thing (which means "assembly") was the basis of the Viking legal structure, bringing peace (and often payment) to wronged parties. Administered by lawspeakers—essentially Viking judges—the Thing was run like a local court, sometimes taking place in a physical courthouse

Established law helped to quell violent blood feuds, once popular between clans.

"Every man who thinks a Thing necessary may have one."

GULATHING'S LAW

← Norse laws were first written down in the winter of 1117–1118.

powers, but it had no actual legal authority to carry out the agreed-upon sentence. That responsibility was left to the families to sort out.

While all land-owning freemen were welcome to weigh in on local disputes and even had a hand in crafting law, not all members of Viking society had such liberal rights. Women were permitted to attend the Thing, but could not officially voice an opinion or influence the decisions of the court. Viking-Age slaves, known as thralls, were worse off. Considered property, they could not participate in any way in the legal process. In fact, if a slave was found guilty of a crime, it was a lord who would receive an often watered-down punishment in his place.

Punishment

In Viking society, money talked—and every deed, both good and bad, had a price. Fines and settlements were a popular punishment for myriad offenses, from thievery to murder. They were levied on the convicted and based on a set fee for the crime. While the richest and most powerful could always "afford" to commit a crime, the cost was at times determined by the accused's ability to pay—a progressive rule in today's society, let alone in the Viking era. And though most crimes could be tried at the local level, fines and penalties could not possibly atone for the most serious of crimes: notably, those illustrating poor moral character.

Alternative Punishment

The fine would be split between the community, the injured party and the chieftain. Some people chose other options. There was limited banishment, which meant the convicted person could not return home for a period of three years. And then there was total banishment, the ultimate price, used almost exclusively for dishonorable crimes. Not only did a banished person have to leave their land and everything they owned, they were considered outside the law and could be killed without retribution. Execution was allowed by the Vikings, but duels were more common. The *holmgang* was a popular type of duel used to

of sorts; sometimes it was simply a gathering of local society members.

The parallels between the modern-day legal system and the Vikings' system were many. The lawspeaker took on a judge-like role. There were no written law books, so they memorized each prior ruling in order to apply precedent to the crime at hand. There was also a jury of peers— that is, freemen aged 12 or older—tasked with deliberation and sentencing.

At the trial, the jury would hear from the accuser and the accused, in addition to relevant witnesses, to paint the clearest picture of the event. The chieftain would weigh in, as would the lawspeaker, whose opinion was held in high regard. If the accused was found guilty, a punishment would be levied. Where their process differs from our own: The Thing had both judiciary and legislative settle disputes. Highly regulated by the Thing, the *holmgang* duel helped to avoid extended blood feuds and murder.

Avoiding Judgment Day

Vikings found many ways around the traditional punishments of the Thing. Many would send another in their place—often a thrall who could not themselves be punished. Women were known to seek assassins or other avenues of private justice on multiple occasions, as they could not stand in court on their own behalf.

And while the Viking legal system wasn't a perfect system—it was flawed like all others—one thing was certain: Though lacking a centralized government, Viking villages and societies were able to come together to create their own structured world, free from chaos. In the process, they built one of the most intricate and effective legal structures of their day, one which lawmakers and scholars have emulated over the course of a millennia.

Another Role

In time, the Thing evolved into not just the legal core, but also the social epicenter of a Viking town. As the Norse people began to develop small villages, instead of segregating by clan, a sense of camaraderie and community needed to be built alongside houses and halls.

The Thing united the people of a region by offering not only a place to deliver judgment, but also a physical meeting place for festivals and holidays, which had previously taken place in private residences.

Politics, community decisions and new laws were also functions of the Thing. Held once or twice a year, these meetings generally lasted several days and brought with them a festive atmosphere crowded with traders, hunters, fishermen and brew masters. At the Thing, friendships were made and marriages arranged. In addition to meting out justice, the Thing was also the social event of the year.

→
Duels—often held on a small island—were a popular way to settle legal disputes.

THEIR STORIED PAST

VIKING HISTORY HAS BEEN RECITED AND CELEBRATED THROUGH THE AGES IN RUNES, POEMS AND STIRRING SAGAS.

Let us set the scene: It is the great mead hall of Magnus Olafsson, aka Magnus the Good, ruler of both Norway and Denmark in the mid-10th century, and the honeyed wine is flowing in great supply. Everybody is content, no one more so than the king himself, who basks in his power and glory. How great are his confidence and self-regard? It is no matter, for the court poet Arnórr has come to increase it tenfold, for he is the realm's premier *skald*, or poet of the valorous deeds of kings, delivering the most highly prized literature of the Viking Age.

"Magnus, hear a mighty poem!" he begins, and suddenly, the room is quiet, although it will soon be punctuated with cries and huzzahs.

"I know none better than thee; I will exalt thy prowess! Every king is far behind thee!" he continues to exclaim, gaining new acclaim with each utterance. Arnórr speaks in verse of Magnus' life, with each highlight a singular one. In battle, "Thou art a true hawk." His recruits weren't exactly slouches either: "No little company didst though gather, for the people of the land sought thee as their liege." And his success was inevitable: "Your enemies trembled, it is said…[and] fled, fearing for their lives." But that was all for naught: Later, fighting the Wends—aka the Slavs in Germanic countries—"Ye did work woe" to the enemy, Arnórr declares, and great was the victory: "There lay there a pile of corpses so high that

↑
A tapestry from the Skogar Museum in Iceland captures a saga scene of beauty and valor.

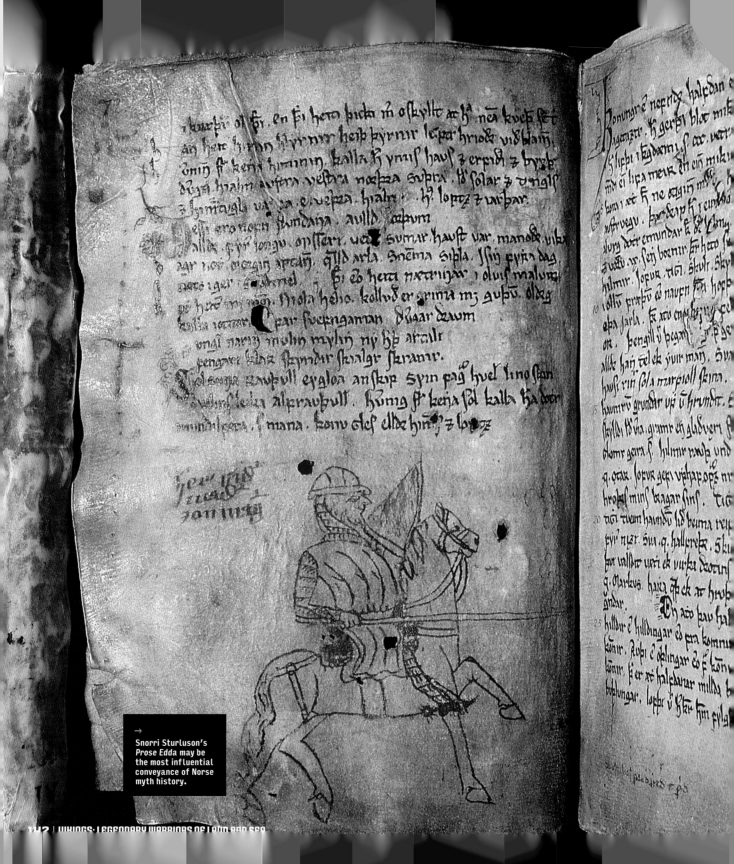

→ Snorri Sturluson's *Prose Edda* may be the most influential conveyance of Norse myth history.

the wood-haunting, wide-roving pack of wolves could not climb it."

Now Arnórr has the crowd—and the "generous" king who will later pay him handsomely—in the palm of his hand. "Thou has given me song, son of Olaf.... A greater king than thee will never be born under the sun!"

Those kinds of superlatives sum up the role of Scandinavian literature both then and now. Such words of praise have united the people with a purpose of understanding, appreciating and celebrating the exploits of kings, warriors and gods both great and just.

The rub, however, is that as writers evolved away from these recited, then recollected poems, and into the more fully written sagas that dominated Viking storytelling beginning in the 12th century, the less the stories contained any semblance of actual fact—not that it has mattered much to the lovers of tales. "Most historians avoid using the so-called historical sagas as sources for the Viking Age," writes Anders Winroth in *The Age of the Vikings*. "The sagas are, nevertheless, wonderful literary texts in their own right, well worth reading for their creative richness and exciting plots."

Character Driven

A great many theories abound regarding the literary life of the Vikings. As per usual, so much of the talk is speculative, fueled by whatever artifacts archaeologists have been able to uncover.

It is known that runes were the first indication of written word among the Scandinavians. The rune language, or *Futhark*—so named for the first six symbols in its alphabet—consists of 24 letters, with each letter also corresponding to a word for ease of use. Those letters were often carved into wood, stone or jewelry, although in wood, it could be difficult to distinguish horizontal lines of the lettering along the grain. The practice is said to have begun in the second century; by the ninth, a 16-letter "Younger" version of the runic language was birthed; the "Elder" alphabet was more formal, while the 16-letter set was

for everyday use. Runes also famously mixed intricate illustrative carvings with lettering to get messages across, as with the huge 10th-century Jelling Stones erected by King Gorm the Old and later by his son Harald Bluetooth in Denmark. In both cases, they read like elaborate, honorific gravestone markings.

How did the runes and the runic language arrive in the first place? Did it come to Scandinavia courtesy of the Etruscan language, or through the Germanic people? Or was it a gift the great god Odin gave them from the world of death after he'd hung upside down in the Yggdrasil tree for nine days, nursing a spear wound? For fans of the pagan peoples, both notions have the ring of the plausible.

The Write Stuff

As with many other cultures, it was the expansion of expression, tools and world exploration—along with the Vikings' well-known taste for

LEGEND HAS IT

Let's see: A series of stories about heroes, villains and gods, a dragon and a tyrant, a queen and some snakes, fire and a hoard of treasure—with all the action concerning a dwarf who lives in a cave under a waterfall who has accrued great wealth, all thanks to a powerful, supernatural ring that can bring terrible tragedy to its bearer. What a precious story that is! And while it may sound like something out of J.R.R. Tolkien, it's actually the tale of Anvari from Norse mythology, which would later inspire the much-celebrated *The Lord of the Rings* books.

adaptation—that helped evolve the telling of Scandinavian history. The skaldic poems had been, for centuries, part of a recited, oral tradition that stressed the power and ethics of leaders. The sagas began to spring up in the 12th century in Iceland, which became ground zero for the encyclopedic creation and preservation of all records of Viking culture, beliefs, heritage and history. That history was founded on the recollection of the poems that had celebrated first the rulers in kings' sagas (*Konungasögur*) and then later the sagas of interfamily feuds and fighting along with explorations and adventures (*Islendingasögur*), and finally, the heroic and wild tales of one-eyed or hammer-tossing mega-gods (*Fornaldarsögur*) that have become Marvel-ously popular today. They all spoke of gold plundered or traded, loves won and lost, rules made and either enforced or broken, worlds explored and conquered, and trust and battle-strength tested on the high seas. They also spoke of Christ rejected or accepted, usually at the threat of death insisted upon by a king who has suddenly seen the light.

Ironically enough, it was the rejection of the pagan culture by the Christians—and the potential loss of a treasure chest of mythological stories—that partly inspired Icelandic writer Snorri Sturluson to take up the quill and begin to record the old stories. Granted, readers were able to see plenty of parallels between the Norse tales and Christian stories and parables, which some felt blurred the belief one might have in the legends. But both old fans and the newly fascinated were drawn in not only by the stories, but also by the drama Snorri infused in them.

No Loss for Words

It would be difficult to overstate Snorri's influence on the propagation of this history. His *Prose Edda* explains the complicated poetic meter used during the Viking Age, along with the compound descriptors, or *kennings*, the oral poets made use of; it also offers up some incredible page-turners of great Norse mythology stories. But it is his

> **"Let them alone, the unshadowed sheer rocks stand/Over the twilight graves of that poor band/ Who count so little in the great world's game!"**
>
> FROM *THE STORY OF GETTIR THE STRONG*

12th-century epic *Heimskringla*, translated as "Circle of the World," that truly shines as a nonstop chronicle of sea wolves' adventures. The many sagas within form a history of the Scandinavian peoples starting with the rule of Norwegian King Harald Fairhair in the ninth century, and ending with the death of Norway's Eystein Meyla, the would-be king, in 1177 after a period of civil war. It contains a multitude of stories (the veracity of which increase the closer they get to Snorri's contemporary time), from a very mortal Odin settling prehistorically in Scandinavia, through St. Olaf's lengthy reign in Norway, and up to and including the tragic Harald Hardrada's epic adventures throughout the lands.

Olaf's first-ever battle, according to the saga, was fought when he was all of 12, but even then he was considered a king since he was defending the honor of his murdered royal father. The young man, according to Snorri (in typically overwritten fashion), had "particularly fine eyes, which were beautiful and piercing, so that one was afraid to look him in the face when he was angry." The account of that first battle, taken from the skalds, revels in drama:

"They launch his ship where waves are foaming—
To the sea shore
Both mast and oar,
And sent his o'er the seas a-roaming.
Where did the sea-king first draw blood?
In the battle shock
At Sote's rock
The wolves howl over their fresh food."

The tragic death of Baldur, "the bleeding god" and son of Odin, is part of the *Poetic Edda*.

Not to be outdone by the legendary characters he fostered, Snorri was himself also a powerful politician, twice elected as "lawspeaker," or head of the Althing parliament proceedings in Iceland. At first a trusted ally of Norway's King Haakon IV, conflicts and bitterness ultimately made Snorri's position untenable, and in a secret plot, he was murdered by royal order in 1241.

In the centuries since, more sagas have been written, and others have been interpreted again and again by translators who were too often motivated to either add ideas or leave notions out, depending upon tales they wished to tell. Some figures have been seen as more or less Christian, or more or less violent. In *The Saga of the Greenlanders*, Leif Erikson discovered the New World; in *The Saga of Erik the Red*, Leif is considered more of a bit player compared to an explorer named Thorfinn Karlsefni—a claim that has long been disputed.

The truth of all the Viking adventures and figures will never be fully known, and archaeological finds throughout the ages have also distorted and re-sorted facts. In a sense, truth is secondary, however, compared to the triumphs of kings and commoners, and the stories that inspire readers even today. As the legendary Norse hero of sagas Ragnar Lothbrok—who may or may not have even been real—says in the popular TV series *Vikings*, "Don't waste your time looking back. You're not going that way."

> **"Brothers shall fight and fell each other, And sisters' sons shall kinship stain..."**
>
> FROM THE *POETIC EDDA, VÖLUSPÁ— THE WISE-WOMAN'S PROPHECY*

↑ One historian said Snorri produced the most important body of Middle Ages literary history.

SNORRI STURLUSON

GOLDEN GEAR

The sagas often speak of stunning goods celebrating gods and victors; here, some notable treasures of the ages.

Through over three centuries as raiders and traders, the Vikings became especially adept at moving goods around from one part of the world to another. And those particular exploits also became the subjects of sagas that were commemorated in examples of wealth that lined the pockets of the gentry and the coffers of warriors, as well as art that honored the most stirring tales of yore. These are a few examples of the goods created by artists or uncovered by archaeologists.

BERSERKER BOOTY

The world's largest collection of Viking silver (weighing 148 pounds) was discovered in 1999 in a farm field in Gotland, Sweden.

HORN OF PLENTY

The Swedish History Museum houses this hoard accrued by a wealthy Viking who probably won his riches in the kind of stories the sagas tell.

SIGURD'S SWORD

In a scene from the epic poem of the famed dragon slayer, Regin the blacksmith mends Sigurd's sword in a carving, now in a Norwegian church.

ODIN'S BIRDS

One of two harness mounts depicting the exaggerated beaks and talons of the god's birds, it was produced in the Baltic island of Gotland.

THE THREE GODS

Odin, Thor and Freyr stand in this Skog Church tapestry. When discovered, the textile work was in the church attic, covering a bridal crown.

CHAPTER 5

LEAVING A RICH LEGACY WORTH EXPLORING

WITH THEIR LANGUAGE,
ARTS AND CULTURE, THE
VIKINGS LEFT A MARK ON
HISTORY THAT IS STILL
WITH US TODAY.

↓
English troops
literally had the
Vikings by the
throat, thanks to
Harald's death.

THE END OF AN ERA

THE VIKING AGE COLLAPSED IN 1066,
BUT ITS INFLUENCE WAS JUST BEGINNING.

HARALD HARDRADA

HAROLD GODWINSON

WILLIAM I

THEY SAY HARALD HARDRADA, THE LAST OF THE GREAT AMBITIOUS VIKING ROYALS WHO RULED NORWAY, STOOD OVER 7 FEET TALL, AND THE ONLY THING THAT COULD SINK HIS SHIP WAS THE WEIGHT OF THE RICHES HE LOADED ABOARD.

They say he and his men fought under the raven banner he named the "Land-Waster," a flag he believed was (and long promoted as) the secret to his enormous power. They say he had every right to assume the throne of England in 1066—hadn't it been promised to the previous Norwegian king, Magnus the Good?—even if Harold Godwinson had already been given the crown.

They say he was vicious—Hardrada meant "Hard Ruler"—and a typically paradoxical Viking:

a pillager of churches who, thanks to his wife's staunch Christianity, also built many of them.

They say a great many things, but the only one we know is true for certain is that on September 25, 1066, Harald and his men did meet the English forces in battle, and Harald's shocking and brutal defeat spelled the end of the Viking era as history has come to paint it.

Their chapter had begun around 300 years prior with the dismantling of a church in Northumbria; it ended 150 miles due south, at Stamford Bridge, Yorkshire. Is there a more fitting final symbol of the age than the sight of Harald, rushing toward the British forces with a battle ax raised high in each hand, getting a swift arrow to the throat?

In fact, there is one other pronouncement history makes for certain: The death of Harald spelled the beginning of the reassessment of the Viking influence upon the world, one that continues to evolve, and be felt proudly, to this day.

"The part they are usually given in this transformation is one of destruction," author Lars Brownworth writes in *The Sea Wolves: A History of the Vikings*. "But although they were violent...the destruction they brought was ultimately creative. As one historian put it, 'The burning of the tars makes for richer soil at the next planting.'"

Split Decisions

When the Viking Age began in 793, the idea that they would one day establish a world-shifting rule had almost a ring of the inevitable. They smacked of an utterly unforeseen uniqueness that their violence could only begin to suggest. Their ships, their clothes, their weapons, laws, bounty and beards all spoke of the quality of abundance, and when they first marched upon the staid European continent, the latter's unpreparedness was historic.

"They maintained this kind of Viking energy," Brownworth explains of the victors. "It was tied in with their footloose love of adventure."

That adventure appeared to be their birthright. Discovering a kind of tired and bloated reign among disorganized rulers throughout Europe,

> ## "Northern Heathendom was not the absence of a culture. Viking[s]...had their own cosmology, their own astronomy, their own gods... and their own notions of how best to live and die."
>
> ROBERT FERGUSON IN *THE VIKINGS: A HISTORY*

they took whatever they could gain for trade and profit; when the getting proved too good to pass up, they turned into an ambushing machine, with individual chiefs making their way toward plunder and splendor—and eventually, rule.

But by the time Harald undertook his infamous trip, Europe had had enough of Viking invasions that spread fear and required Danegeld payments for raiders. And troops and kings were better prepared to deal with any onslaughts.

A Fantastic Downfall

Harald's ambition for English rule came to him late. He was only 15 when he and his half brother, Olaf (later St. Olaf), were forced into exile in the Slavic nations that were then known as Kievan Rus. Harald's 15 years there stood him well, and his military exploits earned him plaudits, wealth and a great many loyal troops.

But after his return and his ascension to the throne in Norway, Harald hoped to gain control of Denmark as well, and spent the next 16 years in near-constant war against the Danish ruler, Sweyn Estridsson. He signed a pact in 1064, having not achieved his aim of victory, and his troops were exhausted.

If adventure was the Viking birthright, after a few centuries, it also proved to be their undoing. Ambition, a head-spinning degree of infighting and a celebration of singular heroics among chiefs and sea mavens led to a historic vulnerability. "For almost 250 years, there was not a significant naval battle in the North Atlantic that wasn't Viking against Viking," says Brownworth. "They just blanket everything."

When Harald set his sights on English King Harold Godwinson's throne—egged on by Harold's exiled brother, Tostig—he set sail with 240 longships carrying 9,000 men and a head full of dreams. Like Canute the Great before him, he would sail to world-unifying glory under the banner of the Land-Waster.

Arriving in York, Harald quickly beat back the local forces, agreed to hostage and surrender terms—and waited as word spread to King Harold of his arrival. It did reach Harold, who immediately marched his own troops north in total secrecy to meet the potential usurper of his kingdom.

When he arrived, he found Harald caught totally unaware; the Norwegian king had even split his troop complement in half and was, strategically, outflanked. It was King Harold himself who greeted the Hard Ruler face to face near the Stamford Bridge, promising his traitor brother Tostig a return to some wealth if he and Harald would withdraw. But the die was cast when King Harold launched an insult toward the Viking ruler, sending fate spiraling forward.

The battle was quickly waged, with Harald inciting his loyal troops by grabbing his axes and pressing forward. Even after Harald was sent to his ugly, gurgling end, his men fought on, but the loss of their leader proved too much, and King Harold utterly dispatched both Tostig and Harald's men with the kind of viciousness the Vikings themselves had once been known for.

For the valiant English king, however, victory's sweetness would be short-lived. Word soon came that Norman King William I was headed his way from France with his own troops and hopes of rule. William swiftly overthrew Harold, and the Norman king—now calling himself William the Conqueror—began his English reign.

Notable Footnote

If the Vikings were suddenly relegated to also-ran status in these battles that would rejigger European rule for decades, it's worth noting that Harald, William and Harold all had Viking blood in their lineage. That said, it's also necessary to note that, with Harald's defeat, few Viking rulers would again attempt to mount an attack upon the southern continent, and all would be repelled without a lasting win. Two generations after

LEGEND HAS IT

Interestingly enough, given all the exaggerations the Icelandic sagas are known for, it is with a description of Harald Hardrada in the famed *Heimskringla* that author Snorri Sturluson chooses to practice some moderation. "King Harald was a great man, who ruled his kingdom well in home concerns," he begins in chapter 36 of *The Saga of Harald Hardrada*. But later he writes, "Many of the feats of his manhood are not here written down. This is owing partly to our uncertainty about them, partly to our wish not to put stories into this book for which there is no testimony. Although we have heard many things talked about, and even circumstantially related, yet we think it better that something may be added to, than that it should be necessary to take something away from our narrative." Then, of course, he goes back to singing his copious praises.

Harald, Norway would be ruled by his grandson Olaf III, aka Olaf the Peaceful.

The Vikings would stay closer to home after this, although "home" still included the trade-route outposts they'd birthed, along with a sensibility that would continue to influence kings and cultures for centuries. Harald's death spelled an end to a movement of violence that had once threatened to cleave the world in two.

The sagas would eventually be written of those days, singing the praises of the long-past sea wolves who'd ruled the waves in their longships and had forged a place in new worlds.

Meanwhile, William the Conqueror readied his own destiny in 1066. But as Scandinavian studies expert Robert Ferguson writes in *The Vikings: A History*, "That is another story, and it is not a Viking story."

"Scandinavians spurred political and social change, which...enabled them to enter the mainstream of European history."

FROM *THE AGE OF THE VIKINGS* BY ANDERS WINROTH

↑

→
After winning the throne, William the Conqueror would rule England for the next 21 years.

THE REAL VIKING FACTS

MEAD? MISTLETOE? MONDAYS? THE MEDIEVAL CLIMATE CRISIS? HERE ARE 20 ALL-TIME TRUE-TO-LIFE NORSE KNOWNS.

THE LITTLE ICE AGE

1 Bluetooth Did the Work

Harald Bluetooth was the king of Denmark for nearly 30 years, from 958 to 986, and in that time, he introduced Christianity to the people and consolidated his rule, bringing the many warring factions together under one name. Thus he inspired the naming of Bluetooth technology, which has also united devices in the same way.

2 Words With Weight

Look up the list of English words with Norse origin and you'll find plenty to inspire the kind of fear the Vikings enjoyed in their raiding

days. Anger. Berserk. Crook. Die. Gun. Haunt. Hell. Knife. Outlaw. Ransack. Rugged. Scare. Slaughter. Slaver: All of these made the eventual cut into English.

3 Words That Carry Even More Weight

The Scandinavians also gave us a vocabulary that would serve us much more fully in peace, love and understanding. The list includes: Awe, axle, bask, bylaw, equip, fellow, give, happy, husband, jolly, law, loan, regret, saga, thrall, trust, wing and perhaps most importantly: wrong.

4 Guaranteed Christmas Kiss

Odin's wife, Frigg, grieved long for the loss of her son Baldur. According to Snorri Sturluson's *Prose Edda*, Baldur was struck by a magic sword that had been fashioned from mistletoe. One version of the legend suggests the gods were able to bring Baldur back to life, with Frigg then declaring mistletoe to be a symbol of love...and therefore, something worth kissing under at the holidays.

5 Worlds Apart

Of the nine worlds mentioned in Norse mythology, only one is fully visible to humans, and that's Midgard, the realm of mankind. One translation of that word is "middle-earth," which explains why J.R.R. Tolkien used it in his popular *The Lord of the Rings* saga.

6 The Vikings Dealt With Their Own Global Warming

The Medieval Warm Period was a "climate anomaly" that lasted some 300 years, overlapping with half of the Viking Age. Was it caused by solar activity? A decrease in volcanic eruptions? Something otherworldly? We do know it wasn't caused by auto fumes eating into the ozone layer, although the effect had some

→ Around 2,500 Viking-era runestones like this one still dot the Swedish landscape.

similarity to what's going on now on Earth. For the Vikings, the net result was supposedly ice-free seas that allowed them deeper explorations and, it is said, the founding of North America. However, the gap was short-lived, as the region's "Little Ice Age" followed and lasted into the 1800s.

7 The Slaves Were En-Thralled

Slavery was abolished in Scandinavia in the mid-14th century, but it was practiced a great deal during the Viking Age (with the word seemingly coming from the Slavs who were captured and sold during medieval times). Viking slaves were known as thralls, a word familiar to fans of the old *Star Trek* series for an episode where fighters from other worlds were held captive on planet Triskelion and called "drill thralls."

8 They Never Wrote Anything Down

Yes, it's true: There were runes everywhere, which amounted to a great deal of how the Vikings expressed themselves "on paper"—or, in this case, carved into stones or wood. But in terms of Viking actions and history, it was up to the much more literary-minded victims of their raids to spell out their "achievements," and they brought terrible drama to the wrath of the conquerors. It would be centuries before the sagas of the Vikings—taken from the poems and oral histories expressed elsewhere—gave some "home team" perspective.

9 A Tour of England Is Also a Tour of Viking Place Names

The Scandinavian language—and the Viking occupation—left its mark on the map of the United Kingdom. Names of towns and cities ending in "–by" (Grimsby, Brondby, Lyngby... there are more than 200 such places in total) owe their nomenclature to the Norse and the Danes, with the suffix translating to mean, essentially, "town." The same also goes for the more than 150 places that end with "-thorpe," which is an Old Norse word for a farm or homestead.

OTHERWORLDLY THRALLS

10 The Days Owe Their Names to the Gods

While the Romans can claim their share of credit when it comes to month names, the Vikings have something of a monopoly on the days of the week. For instance, Tuesday (Tirsdsay) is named for the Norse got Tyr; Wednesday hearkens back to the Middle English "Day of Woden," a variation on Odin, the ultimate among the Norse Age gods; and Thursday is a reference to "Thor's Day."

11 Helmet With Horns? Naaaah

Such headgear was never in use by the Berserkers in the golden age of raiding rage. It actually came several centuries later, in an 1876 production of *Der Ring des Nibelungen*, Richard Wagner's epic music cycle based on the sagas. For that showing, a more Germanic view of horned helmets was used, and for whatever reason, it stuck—and can still be seen in the comic strip *Hägar the Horrible*. Oh, and only Thor's helmet seemed to have wings.

"Despite some pop-culture portrayals, the Vikings prided themselves on personal hygiene, using razors, combs and ear cleaners!"

FROM *THE VINTAGE NEWS*

12 Actually, Most Viking Warriors Didn't Wear Any Helmets

This claim goes beyond the idea that archaeologists have only found one complete Viking helmet (that's the famed Gjermundbu helmet, found in southern Norway in 1943). In fact, helmets were expensive, and the headgear may have been more typically made of leather instead of metal—that is, if the fighters wore helmets at all.

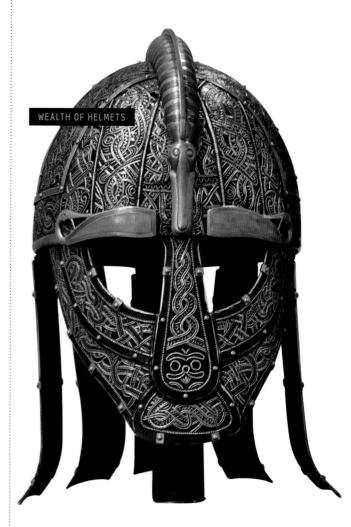

WEALTH OF HELMETS

Frigg and Odin
were important
Scandinavian gods,
but real Vikings
didn't wear horns.

13

13 Let 'em Drink Mead

Poor Kvasir. First, this godly figure was born of the saliva of two groups of other gods. Then, his great wisdom must have made others jealous, for he was killed by two dwarves named Fjalar and Galar, who drained his blood, mixed it with honey and produced a fermented drink that loosened the tongues of poets. The Mead of Poetry, as it was called, has long been produced since then as just mead (although made only with honey, water and other ingredients instead of a god's blood or saliva), and it was enjoyed heartily by the Vikings for centuries.

14 Sea Burials Were Crowded Affairs

Only the wealthiest or most successful folk were given the honor of a sea burial in the tradition of Norse funerals. You would be set adrift in a boat crafted just for this occasion with the finest tools, weapons and ornamental items, as those "grave goods" would help you "on the other side" once you arrived. Also, the dead were often sent on their way accompanied by sacrificed slaves, so the more prominent deceased could have the right kind of help in their heavenly destination. That's one bad fate.

15 Vikings Had a Darwinian Relationship With Their Kids

Babies had best emerge looking fine and strong (and preferably male) if they were meant to have the chance at survival. For a stretch, Scandinavians had an unfortunate habit of tossing youngsters into the surf or simply abandoning them. Infanticide with hardly a second thought was, incredibly, very well embraced during the Middle Ages.

16 They Would Never "Waste" a Fire Starter

In a pinch, for warmth, Vikings would hunt down something called tinder fungus or touchwood found inside tree bark. They'd cut away the outside, thinly slice the inside...and then boil the slices in their own urine. The sodium nitrate in the urine helped make the fires last longer.

17 Who Needs Ribs When You've Got Trees?

According to legend, Man and Woman were born of an ash tree and an elm, respectively, with the great god Odin giving them each life, the god Vili adding consciousness and heart, and Vé offering up hearing and sight. The man, Ask, and the woman, Embla, are the mom and pop of all races on Earth—oh, sorry: Midgard.

DRINKING MEAD

→
A hollowed-out tusk served as a much better pouch for mead than, say, an enemy's skull did.

"Norse people used skis as a means of transportation across the harsh winter terrain, but also as a pastime activity. Even one of the gods they worshipped (Ullr) was devoted to skiing."

FROM *THE VINTAGE NEWS*

18 Skulls Made Bad Cups

Actually, the Vikings wouldn't know: They didn't drink from the skulls of their enemies. Why did we come to think so? Blame some translations of the sagas, which misread the fact that their drinks were actually housed instead in hollowed-out animal tusks.

19 Women Had Power

Beyond the idea that some women were warriors, ladies had unique rights in society. They could request a divorce, inherit property and reclaim their dowry, among other things.

20 Vikings? To You, Maybe

The Vikings never accepted the word "Viking" as a descriptor. That would have meant the people from Norway, Denmark and other Scandinavian countries thought of themselves as one people—and pirates at that. Never happened.

20

SAGAS OF THE

→ Kirk Douglas rides
high as Einar in *The
Vikings*, a film he
also co-produced
(and made a mint on).

SCREEN

FROM COMEDIES AND KIDS FILMS TO EPICS AND OTHERWORLDLY DRAMAS— THESE ARE JUST 10 NOTABLE NORSE FILMS THAT HAVE THRILLINGLY CAPTURED THE OUTSIZED LORE OF THE VIKINGS.

The Vikings 1958

THE PLOT Two Viking half brothers—one a great warrior, the other an ex-slave—compete for a British throne and the love of a beautiful princess.

THAT OH-SO-VIKING DIALOGUE Ragnar Look how he glares at me. If he wasn't fathered by the black ram in the full of the moon my name is not Ragnar. **Ragnar** This is Einar, my only son in wedlock. He's so vain of his beauty, he won't let a man's beard hide it. He scrapes his face like an Englishman. **Einar** Hail Ragnar! And hail Ragnar's beard!

ITS REAL FEEL *The Vikings* was filmed in part in locations in Norway, and based, ultimately, on the sagas of legendary hero Ragnar Lothbrok.

WHY IT RATES This is Golden Age Hollywood's attempt to bring a plunderous story of feasting, drinking and raiding to life, with an all-star cast including Kirk Douglas (Einar), Tony Curtis (Eric), Janet Leigh (Morgana) and Ernest Borgnine (Ragnar). It makes some attempts to capture a sense of accuracy, and Douglas is pretty oar-some as the longship captain.

When the Raven Flies 1985

THE PLOT A classic tale of revenge unfolds when an Irish boy is spared by the Vikings who kill his parents and enslave his sister. Twenty years later, he makes his way to Iceland to exact the price for vengeance, stalking each member of the band of killers like something out of a Clint Eastwood Western.

THAT OH-SO-VIKING DIALOGUE
From the opening of the film's trailer It was in the time of the Vikings that he appeared, like a raven, wandering from place to place, leaving nothing behind him but death. **Thord** You are Christian, that's what is wrong with you!

ITS REAL FEEL This was the first in a trilogy of films by director Hrafn Gunnlaugsson, who updated some plot points from the Vikings' *Sagas of Icelanders* when making it.

WHY IT RATES This acclaimed Icelandic adventure had been submitted by the country for the Best Foreign Language Oscar (it wasn't nominated). Gunnlaugsson touts Sergio Leone's Spaghetti Westerns as inspiration and it shows. In 2016, Icelandic newspaper *Kjarninn* called it the country's best-ever film. It maintains an 84 percent Rotten Tomatoes audience score.

The 13th Warrior 1999

THE PLOT Famed historical scribe Ahmad ibn Fadlan (Antonio Banderas) is sent on a diplomatic mission and, when intercepted by a group of Vikings, is coerced into becoming the last among 13 warriors who must vanquish an "angel of death"—an evil so powerful, even the brave won't name it. At first insulted by his fellow warriors, the writer wins them over on their tragic mission with his bravery and cunning.

THAT OH-SO-VIKING DIALOGUE Ahmad ibn Fadlan [*When handed a Viking sword*] I cannot lift this. **Herger the Joyous** Grow stronger.

ITS REAL FEEL The film is based on Michael Crichton's novel *Eaters of the Dead*, which itself was based on both *Beowulf* and 10th-century writer Ahmad ibn Fadlan's tales of the Volga Vikings, who ruled the area that Russia, Ukraine and Belarus now occupy.

WHY IT RATES It didn't at the time of its release. Although it carried an "A-" rating from *Entertainment Weekly* into a fine opening weekend, the film ultimately did poorly at the box office. And yet, its exhilarating action and atmosphere help it rise above typical action fare, and it offers a compelling Viking narrative.

→
Banderas (right) plays a writer who witnessed the Vikings firsthand.

→
Nicolas Cage and
Tom Hulce were
asked, but Tim
Robbins (right)
won the title role.

Erik the Viking 1989

THE PLOT "From the pages of history…the missing chapter" promises the trailer of this Monty Python-esque adventure (written and directed by troupe member Terry Jones, who wrote a children's book with a similar title…and an utterly different plot). Here, Tim Robbins plays a reluctant Viking who adventures to Valhalla to ask the gods to end the age of violence. Co-stars include Jones, John Cleese and *Downton Abbey*'s Samantha Bond.

THAT OH-SO-VIKING DIALOGUE Helga Why do you have to go around killing and looting all the time? **Erik** To pay for the next expedition, of course. **Helga** But that's a circular argument! If the only reason for the expedition is the killing and looting and the only reason for the killing and looting is to pay for the next expedition, they cancel each other out. **Erik** Stop talking as if we were married!

ITS REAL FEEL Well…it has character names such as Erik, Freya, Aud, Sven the Berserk, Ivar the Boneless and Leif the Lucky. And Jones' British comic fantasy is based at least in part on Norse mythology.

WHY IT RATES Famed critic Roger Ebert may have hated it, but it was comic master Jones' attempt to turn the dramatic tables on Viking myths. Much of it lands well, making it a worthy entry in the canon.

Danish strongman Thorsen had prior sword experience in two *Conan* films in the 1980s.

bodybuilders Ralf Moeller and Sven-Ole Thorsen play Kjartan and Gunnar, respectively).

WHY IT RATES One line Magnus the Lawgiver delivers in the film—"I can tell you: You must never kill twice in the same family"—comes straight from *Njál's Saga*, which serves as at least some inspiration for this film that captures the violence and contentiousness of the age.

Trees Grow on the Stones, Too 1985

THE PLOT When young Kuksja survives a Viking attack on his Russian village, the pagans believe he's their good luck charm. They cart him along and he grows into a powerful and valiant warrior, so much so that he's adopted by the chief, Torir, and renamed Einar. But when he falls for the gorgeous Signy, real trouble begins.

THAT OH-SO-VIKING DIALOGUE Torir Don't stand up against the gods, Sigurd! Odin has sent us the boy alive. The lord of the undead himself did not want him to drown. Nor your sword or the sea mouth could bite him. **Einar** [*Discovering his weapon locked in storage*] Einar's sword—my sword. Why is it here? **Torir** You came to us with peace. Therefore, your weapons are here—just in case!

ITS REAL FEEL Spectacular Norwegian scenery, some realistic-looking longship sword action and nice sets speak well for a film that found co-directors Knut Andersen and Stanislav Rostotsky trying to bring a taste of Wild West action to their Norse drama.

WHY IT RATES Some Norwegian critics disparaged this Soviet co-production at the time, but it does manage to be both Viking adventure film and somewhat more family-friendly fare.

The Viking Sagas 1995

THE PLOT The plot does, in fact, sound straight out of the sagas (crossed with the sensibility of a video game), as the mythical warrior Kjartan takes on the evil Vikings who hope to keep him from marrying the woman he loves, inheriting his father's land and fulfilling his destiny.

THAT OH-SO-VIKING DIALOGUE Gunnar [*Tapping a napping Kjartan with his sword*] Is that how Valgard died? Did Ketil find your father asleep? **Kjartan** [*Waking up enraged*] My father wrapped his guts around a stone so I could escape and find you! **Gunnar** I hope you are as brave as he was.

ITS REAL FEEL Filmed mostly in Iceland with a cast of locals (Viking film actors/competitive

Outlander 2008

THE PLOT That's right: It's a Viking-era adventure drama...*and* a science-fiction fantasy. A spacecraft crash-lands in pre-Viking-era Scandinavia, and the lone human aboard, Kainan (Jim Caviezel), is captured by the local king's troops and dubbed an outlander. Unfortunately, Kainan has unwittingly brought an alien enemy along: a predator called the Moorwen. Can Kainan join his space-age tech with the Vikings' Iron Age weapons to do battle? And more to the point: Between Kainan and the Moorwen, which of the otherworldly combatants is truly the more evil one?

THAT OH-SO-VIKING DIALOGUE Freya All of the women are talking about you. They say you're from a place far beyond the ice. I heard one say—from the home of the gods. **Kainan** What do you think? **Freya** I think she was a little drunk.

ITS REAL FEEL The film is based in part on *Beowulf*, and King Hrothgar in the epic poem is echoed in the same-named character in this film.

WHY IT RATES Like too many a Viking-related film, *Outlander* didn't have nearly as many fans upon its release as it does now; it has become a true cult classic, in part because of its fine cast and terrific special effects.

"[Jim Caviezel] liked that the film had Christian parallels. That was not our intent; it's how he read it."

OUTLANDER DIRECTOR HOWARD McCAIN

→ A replica Viking village, along with a longship, were constructed to make *Outlander*.

Valhalla Rising 2009

THE PLOT Who exactly is this supernaturally strong, heavily tattooed slave named One Eye? Despite the injury that gave him his name, the mute warrior begins to see his destiny as he breaks free of his captors, boards a Viking vessel and heads toward the Holy Land in this 11th-century adventure of sacrifice, hardship and resurrection.

THAT OH-SO-VIKING DIALOGUE Eirik Where does he come from? **Kare** He was brought up from hell…. **Eirik** And where is this hell? **Kare** On the other side of the ocean.

ITS REAL FEEL This Danish period drama, filmed entirely in Scotland, takes place in 1096, just past the end of the Viking Age, but it well covers the grudging struggle between paganism and Christianity.

WHY IT RATES That Mads Mikkelsen (below) is magnetic as One Eye explains at least part of the film's evolving appeal. A Rotten Tomatoes positive rating of 71 percent also speaks to the film's visual majesty, cinematic carnage and cult status.

→
Jay Baruchel has voiced Hiccup in all three *Dragon* films, as well as an animated TV series.

How to Train Your Dragon 2010

THE PLOT In a remote Viking village, Hiccup, the 15-year-old son of Stoick, a brave dragon slayer, dreams of following in his father's footsteps. But when he inadvertently hurts one of the dangerous Night Fury dragons, he comes to discover that friendship is a saner way to stop the bitterness between humans and the majestic creatures.

THAT OH-SO-VIKING DIALOGUE Stoick My father told me to bang my head against a rock and I did it! I thought I was crazy, but I didn't question him. And you know what happened? **Gobber** You got a headache. **Stoick** That rock split in two! It taught me what a Viking can do, Gobber! He can crush mountains, level forests, tame seas! Even as a boy, I knew what I was, what I had to become…. Hiccup is not that boy.

ITS REAL FEEL Leave it to DreamWorks to find a way to perhaps inadvertently chronicle the Vikings' method of relating after raiding.

WHY IT RATES Retooling a violent historical story through big-budget animation (*The Hunchback of Notre Dame*, *Pocahontas*) has worked before, but rarely this well. *Dragon* spawned two sequels; all three were nominated for Best Animated Feature at the Academy Awards.

←
One Eye (played by Mads Mikkelson, center) was also a nickname for the god Odin.

Thor 2011

THE PLOT He's all-powerful...and he knows it! He may be the God of Thunder, but Thor (Chris Hemsworth) is a bit of a hammerhead when it comes to understanding what his father, Odin (Anthony Hopkins), expects of him. Being cast out of Asgard and sent to Earth helps him lose his historic arrogance and turns him into a great, compassionate defender.

THAT OH-SO-VIKING DIALOGUE Young Thor When I am king, I'll hunt the monsters down and slay them all! Just as you did, Father! **Odin** A wise king never seeks out war. But he must always be ready for it. [*He walks off and his sons follow.*] **Young Thor** I'm with you, Father! **Young Loki** So am I! **Odin** Only one of you can ascend to the throne. But *both* of you were born to be kings!

ITS REAL FEEL Telling the story of the Viking gods—and the famed Marvel comics story birthed by the legendary Stan Lee—allows for all the spectacle of violence for heroics' sake.

WHY IT RATES Part of the Marvel film franchise's master plan was to bring Thor and half brother Loki into the fold of superheroes. The tales have not disappointed; this film earned $449.3 million and spawned three sequels.

"Brother, however I have wronged you, I am sorry. But these people are innocent; taking their lives will gain you nothing. So take mine!" THOR

JELLING STONES

THE ULTIMATE

THE LUSH BEAUTY OF DISTANT LANDS? THE WONDERS OF

LURE OF THE LORE A mix of museums and remade longships brings you closer to a Viking stronghold where rulers were made and wealth was spread.

SIGHTS YOU'LL POST ABOUT It's fitting to start in what was once the oldest city in Denmark, and where commerce was king. The **Hedeby Viking Museum** in Schleswig-Holstein by the Jutland Peninsula is across from the seminal trade settlement founded by King Godfrid. You'll find a wealth of archaeological discovery, and nearby, reconstructed Viking houses. Gorm the Old and his son Harald Bluetooth had the carved memorial Jelling stones with runic inscriptions built, each standing about 36 feet high, in **Jelling**, in the south-central town of Vejle. North of that in Hobro, **Fyrat** was established during Harald's reign, and now has nine reconstructed houses, a fascinating

ring fort and a cemetery. Meanwhile, over 700 graves of a variety of sizes and shapes can be found in the Iron Age graveyard in **Lindholm Hoje**, in the northern Denmark city of Aalborg, and a nearby museum offers finds and tales.

On nearby Zealand Island, just west of Copenhagen in the town of Roskilde, the **Viking Ship Museum** features five huge reconstructed longships dating back over 1,000 years. Originally excavated in 1962, the five ships had been sunk purposely to protect the local inlet. A more impressive fortification can be found in the famed **Trelleborg Ring Castle** in Slagelse, on Zealand Island. The tale of the giant circular structure can be found at museums both in Slagelse and Copenhagen. And on the Danish island of Funen, the **Ladby Burial Ship** in Kurteminde's Viking Museum dates back to approximately 925. *visitdenmark.com*

VIKING SHIP MUSEUM

HEDEBY VIKING MUSEUM

LADBY BURIAL SHIP

DENMARK

VIKING VACATION

THE ANCIENT WORLD? YOU CAN TRAVEL TO SEE WHERE IT ALL HAPPENED.

ICELAND

LURE OF THE LORE Swim in hot springs in a cold climate as the Vikings once did, and experience their farm life firsthand.

SIGHTS YOU'LL POST ABOUT Many of this land's Viking attractions can be found out west, starting in the capital of Reykjavík. The **National Museum of Iceland** begins its history with the Viking settlements (and features the ship they came in on). For a deeper dive, the underground **Settlement Exhibition** is built around an archaeological dig and includes the oldest remains of human habitation in the city, dating to the ninth century.

Since the Vikings were devoted to their tales as no other civilization is, the **Saga Museum** lets you in on some of their compelling stories, with re-creations of key moments. A number of those tales were spun by the legendary 13th-century scribe and politician Snorri Sturluson. Snorri may have been killed in a tunnel in the village of Reykholt—which sits northwest of Reykjavík—but the real attraction here is the **Snorralaug**, a nearby geothermic hot pool. Snorri, like the Vikings he wrote of, once bathed here—a practice you can participate in as well.

Viking World, near Reykjavík in Keflavík, offers up a replica of *The Icelander*, a ninth-century ship; you can even wander beneath the hull. Also in western Iceland's Dalabyggð region, the **Eiriksstadir Living Museum** contains a

replica of Erik the Red's home and farm, which is where Leif Erikson was born.

In northern Iceland, the **Glaumbaer Turf House** contains a dozen buildings in an area carefully preserved since 874. The turf houses were the most popular living style of the day, and the Glaumbaer, a protected site since 1947, is now under the control of the National Museum of Iceland. *inspiredbyiceland.com*

EIRIKSSTADIR LIVING MUSEUM

SETTLEMENT EXHIBITION

VIKING WORLD

NATIONAL MUSEUM OF ICELAND

NORWAY

LURE OF THE LORE The most impressive of all Viking ships you can see is in this beautiful country.

SIGHTS YOU'LL POST ABOUT Oslo is Norway's capital city, and like Reykjavík in Iceland, it is home to both some of the most stirring moments in Winter Olympics history, and to the glorious and golden conquests of the Vikings as well. It's in Oslo that you'll find the **Viking Ship Museum**, which houses the breathtaking Oseberg ship, the real-life relic that looks like the Viking vessels of popular imagination. Dating from around 800 and discovered in a large burial mound south of the city near Tønsberg (alongside two female skeletons), it stretches over 70 feet long and 16 feet wide. The oak ship has everything: the intricately carved and curled wooden decorations at stem and stern; a 30-foot mast; and intricate details. The exhibit is part of the country's **Museum of Cultural History**, which has some of its own valued archaeological finds.

Head farther southwest to the Rogaland County town of Avaldsnes and you'll be privy to the picturesque **Viking Farm**—a can't-miss for any Viking-phile. Here's your chance to really get in on life in the old settlement, on a plot that was built specifically as part of an experimental archaeological research program surveying the way folks went about their lives back in the ninth century. Weaponry, cooking, hunting, culture and more can be explored in an area the local website describes as being "on a small, forested island, just inside the rocks where King Olaf Tryggvason drowned a group of wizards one thousand years ago." Forgoing that fate, you can walk along by the farmyard with its longhouse, and the boat house built for a warship.

And up north in the Nordland County on Vestagoya among the Lofoten Islands, the **Lofotr Viking Museum** can be found on a site where, in 1983, archaeologists discovered a **Chieftain's House**. The home was later reconstructed for touring—complete with the Viking tools for cooking and killing. The original home, at 272 feet long and 30 feet high, remains the largest Viking-era house discovered. At that size, what took so long to find it? *visitnorway.com*

VIKING SHIP MUSEUM

AVALDSNES VIKING FARM

CHIEFTAIN'S HOUSE

LOFOTR VIKING MUSEUM

← The Oseberg ship includes elaborately carved designs in its wood.

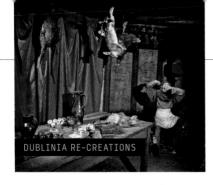
DUBLINIA RE-CREATIONS

DUBLINIA MUSEUM

JORVIK VIKING CENTRE

LINDISFARNE PRIORY

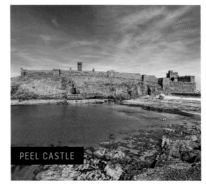
PEEL CASTLE

THE BRAAID

BRITISH ISLES

LURE OF THE LORE For three centuries, the Vikings held their own in European capitals—and here's a vision of how they left them.

SIGHTS YOU'LL POST ABOUT Time to hail the conquering heroes? Well, with centuries having passed, tourist attractions throughout the U.K. give a glimpse of the complicated history between the Norsemen and the British Kingdom. We start in the northeast, and the famed Northumberland spot near Newcastle upon Tyne, where the Vikings first raided. The **Lindisfarne Priory** offers beautiful island views and sights of the monastery ruins of yore. Heading south, York has the **Jorvik Viking Centre**, housing the reconstruction of a Viking city from around the year 975. (Slightly eerie detail: The reconstruction includes figures whose size is based on skulls found near the site.) Carriages take you past dioramas depicting Viking life, from craft-making to ironworks.

The Isle of Man, situated between the U.K. and Northern Ireland, has its own proud Viking heritage, from homesteads to monuments to famed archaeological digs. **Peel Castle**, set on St. Patrick's Island, was originally a place of worship that ended up a fortress for 11th-century King Magnus Barelegs. The place offers incomparable views above and atmospherically creepy crypts below, with extensive grounds and gatehouse towers. **The Braaid** brings together Iron Age and Viking architecture in a Norse roundhouse and farm settlement.

No such visit would be complete without touring Ireland to see the incredible impact of the Vikings, who first invaded in 795 before their lengthy stay. Dublin's **Dublinia** opens the modern world to medieval and Viking Dublin, including a museum with Viking relics (check out the moss toilet paper), performers reenacting historic moments from days past (watch out for the weapons), and a stroll down what would have been a bustling Viking street (keep an eye out for the Viking toothache remedies). And in nearby Waterford, the **Viking Triangle** got its name because of walls Norsemen once built. Now you can see a replica of a longship, and visit the noted **Reginald's Tower** museum to see Viking treasures. *visitbritain.com; ireland.com*

GREENLAND

LURE OF THE LORE

It's where Erik the Red came ashore, gave the land its cockeyed name and built a culture (for a time).

SIGHTS YOU'LL POST ABOUT

Speaking of the country's founder, you can find a reconstruction of **Erik the Red's Longhouse**, built in Brattahlid, the southwestern estate he populated (now known as Qassiarsuk), and where his son Leif Erikson was born. While it's historically impressive, it arguably pales next to the nearby **Tjodhilde's Church** re-creation, honoring the first Christian church built (by Erik's wife, after her conversion) on the continent. It also helps tourists recall her difficulty in convincing Erik to do the same, after reputedly promising to cut off marital relations until the big switch. The church is small, but can still hold 20 to 25 worshippers. And in nearby Qaqortoq, you'll find the impressive ruins of the 14th-century **Hvalsey Church**, with 20-foot stone walls still rising up above the coastal settlement. *visitgreenland.com*

ERIK'S LONGHOUSE

TJODHILDE'S CHURCH

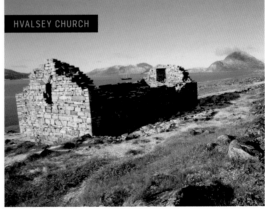

HVALSEY CHURCH

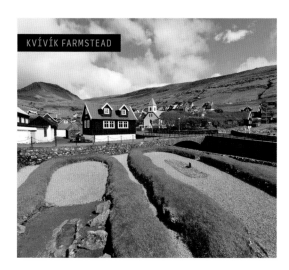
KVÍVÍK FARMSTEAD

HISTORICAL MUSEUM

TOFTANES FARMSTEAD

LURE OF THE LORE

They didn't plunder the place; they plotted settlements here instead, and left a legacy along the blissful archipelago.

SIGHTS YOU'LL POST ABOUT Central among the 18 islands that make up this Danish territory between Iceland and Norway is the riverside city of Kvívík on the island of Streymoy, which contains a unique **Viking Farmstead**. The longhouse is indeed long—72 feet by 20 feet wide—and inside, it contains a narrow 23-foot firepit that had once been used for heating and cooking. The large nearby barn is also unique to the islands. Cross a narrow channel by bridge and you come to the village of Leirvik (on the island of Eysturoy), which is where you'll find **Toftanes**, a farmstead that also dates back 1,000 years and has its own 72-foot longhouse with double-built walls for insulation. Both longhouses, when excavated, produced thousands of artifacts, which you can now find on view at the **Historical Museum** in the islands' capital city of Tórshavn. *visitfaroeislands.com*

THE FAROE ISLANDS

CANADA

NORSTEAD VILLAGE

LURE OF THE LORE Forget Columbus: The Vikings discovered North America, and here's your chance to see the landing spot.

SIGHTS YOU'LL POST ABOUT From small things, big things one day come. Case in point: In 1968, archaeologists Helge and Anne Stine Ingstad found a small cloak pin that proved Leif Erikson had made his way to **L'Anse aux Meadows**, discovering the uppermost tip of Canada's Great Northern Peninsula and naming the town in Newfoundland and Labrador "Vinland." You can walk in the steps of the Vikings amid the lush scenery around what are now ancient ruins and a re-created trio of 11th-century wood-framed Viking houses. Finds from the many digs are housed at the nearby interpretive center. Not too far away is the replicated port of **Norstead**, with its 54-foot re-creation of the Viking knarr longship that Leif used to sail from Greenland. All kinds of activities are open to the Vik-curious here, from the quieter pursuits, such as watching yarn being spun, to the more warrior-worthy: sitting in a chieftain's chair, holding a sword or learning how to throw an ax. And, presumably, how to duck! *newfoundlandlabrador.com*

NORSTEAD TRAIL

Norstead

L'ANSE AUX MEADOWS

BIRKA

FEMALE VIKING WARRIOR

TRELLEBORG RING FORTRESS

SWEDEN

LURE OF THE LORE It's a place to explore Viking trade successes, visit a unique fortification and argue about whether women were warriors, too.

SIGHTS YOU'LL POST ABOUT A great many Viking expeditions took off from Sweden, which helps explain why you'll find the **Trelleborg Ring Fortress** in the southern tip of the country. Most of these distinctively circular forts are found in Denmark, but Trelleborg fits the profile, built in the 980s and with a similar number and style of buildings. The re-creation is worth a look, as is the town of **Birka**, which sits in the southeast part of the country, just west of Stockholm. Once a seed of Northern European trade, Birka now has Viking home reconstructions and special events. It also, famously, is the burial site of the **Birka Female Viking Warrior**, who, until a 2017 DNA study, was thought to be a male fighter. The discovery has shed a new, controversial light on gender roles in Viking society. The accompanying artifacts prove she was quite the pro when it came to swordplay. *visitsweden.com*

THE SUPREME SEA QUEST

HOW WILL YOU DO ON
OUR VIKING TRIVIA QUIZ?
WILL YOU BE A PILLAGER—
OR A PRETENDER?

1 **The Viking longships were classics of design, but how far could they travel in a day?**
A 50 miles
B 90 miles
C 125 miles
D 300 miles

2 **Where did the Vikings believe the best of them would head to when they died?**
A Avalon
B Tartarus
C Valhalla
D Niflheim

3 **What kind of birds would you find sitting at Odin's throne?**
A Pigeons
B Seagulls
C Owls
D Ravens

4 **By what age were Viking children considered grown?**
A 8
B 12
C 14
D 18

THE REGAL ODIN

↑
How far could the
mighty longships
travel, and what
technique was used
to make them?

5 **What was the name of the shipbuilding technique used by the Vikings to create their longships?**
A Clinker
B Trireme
C Helming
D Carrack

6 **Norse legend tells us the sun and the moon are always in a great hurry—why?**
A Each new day carries the promise of adventure
B Because Odin set them at odds against each other
C They're the original berserkers
D They're being chased by wolves

7 **Which of these statements is *not* true about the longhouses built during the Viking Age?**
A They could be as long as about 250 feet
B Fires to provide light, heat and a means for cooking were either built in the central aisle in the house or in in-room firepits
C Humans and animals sheltered together
D They were filled with furniture and the beds were the most elaborate parts

8 **Which of these descriptions is NOT true of the impressive Viking longships?**
A Their hulls' shallow draft design made them less likely to tip in strong winds
B The carved animal-head embellishments at the front of the ships were meant to strike fear in the enemy
C They were adept at sailing through very shallow waters
D The longships almost never took on water

9 **Traditionally, among the Vikings, which would be the first meal of each day?**
A Nattmal
B Dagmal
C Veltum
D Apetaval

10 **The game of *hnútukast* involved which of the following?**
A An early version of tug-o-war
B A bat made of some kind of hard metal called a Knattle
C A version of dodgeball that used leftover bones from a meal to maximize injury
D Skis similar to those we use today

11 **What is the name of Thor's hammer?**
A Jord
B Baldurnik
C Mjölnir
D Mimir

12 **Following a feast, what did the Vikings have for dessert?**
A Pudding
B Fresh-baked cookies
C Nothing—they didn't like dessert
D Honey

13 **Which Viking god travels in a chariot drawn by two male cats named Bygul and Trjegul?**
A Freyja
B Odin
C Aegir
D Tyr

14 **Which day of the week doesn't have a naming association with the Vikings?**
A Tuesday
B Wednesday
C Thursday
D Saturday

15 **In Njál's Saga, which is NOT true of Gunnar?**
A He can leap higher than his own height with his armor on
B He swims like a seal
C He carries a spear called an atgeir
D He is dark-haired and dark-eyed

→ This heavenly looking spot is where the Vikings went after death—what is it called?

16 Which of these statements about raiding is true?

A It was considered by the Vikings to be the same as thievery

B It was a full-time occupation; in Viking culture, you were either a raider or a farmer or something else

C Raiding was not a desirable occupation, and many warriors had to be drafted into service by chieftains

D It increased your status and made it easier to get a bride

17 How did Odin lose an eye?

A He was impaled on a branch at Yggdrasil in order to learn the secret of the runes

B It was the cost of drinking from Mímir's fountain, which made him all-wise

C He lost it in battle with his son Loki

D It was given to the oracle, allowing the Vikings to see the future

18 Who was Ullr?

A The slayer of Erik the Red

B Author of two of the most famous Icelandic sagas

C The first conqueror of York

D The god of skiing and archery

19 Of the Jarls, Karls and Thralls, which class was the lowest in Nordic society?

A Jarls

B Karls

C Thralls

D The Jarls and Karls were of equal status

20 What is the one right Viking women did not have?

A They could own property

B They could hold political power alongside men

C They could legally divorce their husbands

D They could collect an inheritance

21 A Thing is a public assembly where legal disputes were settled among the Vikings. But what is an Althing?

A A place for Christmas celebrations and mead drinking

B The name for the Icelandic parliament building

C An altar where marriage ceremonies were conducted

D The proceeding through which criminals were banished for two years at a time

22 What was regarded as "flyting" in Viking culture?

A An ancient-era "rap battle" of sorts where poets exchanged insults

B The kind of high-level berserker battle action told of in the sagas

C A medieval kind of fly-fishing used to catch salmon in Denmark

D A particular type of trade practiced between warring parties

23 According to Norse myth, which god always chooses justice over vengeance?

A Gefjon

B Thor

C Forseti

D Odin

24 The TV series *Vikings* makes a few interesting historical leaps. Which of these *Vikings* plotlines is actually true?

A Ragnar Lothbrok and Rollo were really brothers

B Ragnar and Rollo were both present at the famed raid on Lindisfarne in 793

C Ragnar was married to Aslaug

D Count Odo was just as weirdly lurid as the show suggests, and he died violently

25 Canute the Great was, at times, ruler of which countries?

A England and Norway

B Norway and Denmark

C Denmark and England

D All three

26 Why did Erik the Red decide not to lead his son Leif's expedition to the New World?

A He was retired

B His wife was pregnant and he didn't want to miss the birth

C He fell off his horse and saw it as a bad omen

D He wanted his son to prove his mettle and venture on his own

VIKINGS' ROLLO

VIKINGS' RAGNAR

↑
Canute had himself one heck of a crown, but how many kingdoms did he rule over?

29 **What modern technology is named after a famed Viking?**
A VirtualShip
B Blockchain
C Bluetooth
D Internet of Things

30 **What is the name given to the fighting force led by Ragnar's sons?**
A Great Heathen Army
B Norse Force
C Berserkers
D Vessel of Vengeance

1C, 2C, 3D, 4B, 5A, 6D, 7D, 8D, 9B, 10C, 11C, 12D,
13A, 14D, 15D, 16D, 17B, 18D, 19C, 20B, 21B, 22A,
23C, 24C, 25D, 26C, 27B, 28B, 29C, 30A

ARE YOU A TRUE SEA WOLF OR A COMMON SHEEP? LET'S SEE HOW WELL YOU DID...

0-12 Correct
You may have to die by the blood eagle for so poor a performance.

13-20 Correct
There surely won't be any sagas written about you anytime soon.

21-25 Correct
A thousand men will follow you into battle on their longships.

26-30 Correct
There should be statues erected of you throughout Scandinavia!

27 **The Elder Futhark system of runes has 24 letters; how many characters does the Younger Futhark system have?**
A 12
B 16
C 26
D 52

28 **What year is commonly associated with the end of the Viking age?**
A 858
B 1066
C 1280
D 1491

Getty Images **86-87** OlegDoroshin/Shutterstock; Bettmann/Getty Images **88-89** Werner Forman/
Getty Images; PRISMA ARCHIVO/Alamy Stock Photo; PHAS/Getty Images **90-91** Universal History
Archive/Getty Images; Werner Forman/Getty Images; DEA/G. DAGLI ORTI/Getty Images **92-93** Print
Collector/Getty Images; MOLA/Getty Images; Print Collector/Getty Images **94-95** WikiMedia
Commons **96-97** WikiMedia Commons; Werner Forman Archive/Shutterstock (2); PRISMA ARCHIVO/
Alamy Stock Photo; WikiMedia Commons **98-99** Heritage Images/Getty Images **100-101** Maria
Heyens/Alamy Stock Photo; Werner Forman Archive/Shutterstock **102-103** Werner Forman Archive/
Shutterstock (2); Heritage Images/Getty Images; Print Collector/Getty Images **104-105** Werner Forman/
Getty Images; Werner Forman/Shutterstock **106-107** Werner Forman/Shutterstock (2); Werner Forman/
Getty Images; Photo 12/Getty Images **108-109** REDA&CO/Getty Images **110-111** Hulton Archive/
Getty Images **112-113** GeorgeBurba/Getty Images **114-115** Botastock images/Alamy Stock Photo;
Getty Images **116-117** Bildagentur-online/Getty Images; Universal History Archive/Getty Images;
Robert Matton AB/Alamy Stock Photo **118-119** De Luan/Alamy Stock Photo; Cindy Hopkins/
Alamy Stock Photo; Print Collector/Getty Images **120-121** Panther Media GmbH/Alamy Stock
Photo **122-123** dpa picture alliance/Alamy Stock Photo; PRISMA ARCHIVO/Alamy Stock Photo;
DEA/G. DAGLI ORTI/Getty Images; Print Collector/Getty Images **124-125** Wolfgang Kaehler/Getty
Images; Panther Media GmbH/Alamy Stock Photo; Werner Forman/Getty Images **126-127** Alfredo
Dagli Orti/Shutterstock; Sergiy1975/Shutterstock **128-129** The Art Archive/Shutterstock; Getty
Images **130-131** Heritage Images/Getty Images; Heritage Images/Getty Images **132-133** Heritage
Images/Getty Images **134-135** Ar2r/Shutterstock; PHAS/Getty Images; Dja65/Shutterstock
136-137 arturbo/Getty Images; Irina Sokolovskaya/Shutterstock **138-139** The History Collection/
Alamy Stock Photo **140-141** Stefan Auth/imageBROKER/Shutterstock **142-143** Werner Forman/
Getty Images **144-145** CPA Media Pte Ltd/Alamy Stock Photo **146-147** Geography Photos/Getty
Images; Heritage Image Partnership Ltd/Alamy Stock Photo; Ajax News & Feature Service/Alamy Stock
Photo; Werner Forman/Getty Images (2); DEA PICTURE LIBRARY/Getty Images **148-149** Lorado/
Getty Images **150-151** WikiMedia Commons **152-153** WikiMedia Commons; Chronicle/Alamy Stock
Photo; Print Collector/Getty Images **154-155** WikiMedia Commons **156-157** Oleksandr Rybitskiy/
Shutterstock; Peter Barritt/Alamy Stock Photo **158-159** Mats O Andersson/Shutterstock; Everett
Collection **160-161** WikiMedia Commons (2) **162-163** Michael Nicholson/Getty Images; Wiki
Commons; Piotr Majka/Shutterstock **164-165** Everett Collection **166-167** Everett Collection;
Orion Pictures/Everett Collection **168-169** Courtesy of The History Channel; Weinstein Company/
Everett Collection **170-171** IFC Films/Everett Collection; Universal Pictures/Everett Collection;
Paramount Pictures/Everett Collection **172-173** Stefano Ember/Shutterstock; Hemis/Alamy Stock
Photo; Don Douglas/Alamy Stock Photo; Leslie Garland Pictures/Alamy Stock Photo; WikiMedia
Commons; ARCTIC IMAGES.Alamy Stock Photo; Travellinglight/Alamy Stock Photo; Yvette Cardozo/
Alamy Stock Photo **174-175** Marka/Getty Images; Richard Cavalleri/Shutterstock; RPBaiao/
Shutterstock; Allen Furmanski/Shutterstock; Print Collector/Gettyb Images; Universal Images
Group North America LLC / DeAgostini/Alamy Stock Photo; Dave Head/Shutterstock; Shutterstock;
Michael Runkel/imageBROKER/Shutterstock; parkerphotography/Alamy Stock Photo; WikiMedia
Commons **176-177** REDA&CO/Getty Images; Prisma by Dukas Presseagentur GmbH/Alamy
Stock Photo; Bildagentur Zoonar GmbH/Shutterstock; imageBROKER/Alamy Stock Photo;
robertharding/Alamy Stock Photo (2) **178-179** robertharding/Alamy Stock Photo; mauritius images
GmbH/Alamy Stock Photo; WendyCotie/Shutterstock; Anders Blomqvist/Alamy Stock Photo;
PRISMA ARCHIVO/Alamy Stock Photo; Nina Alizada/Shutterstock **180-181** WikiMedia Commons;
Nawrocki/ClassicStock/Getty Images **182-183** Alfredo Dagli Orti/Shutterstock **184-185** PictureLux/
The Hollywood Archive/Alamy Stock Photo (2); whitemay/Getty Images **BACK COVER** Peyker/
Shutterstock; Bettmann/Getty Images; Chronicle/Alamy Stock Photo **INSIDE BACK COVER** Alfredo
Dagli Orti/Shutterstock

CENTENNIAL BOOKS

An Imprint of
Centennial Media, LLC
40 Worth St., 10th Floor
New York, NY 10013, U.S.A.

CENTENNIAL BOOKS is a trademark of Centennial Media, LLC

ISBN 978-1-951274-34-4

Distributed by
Simon & Schuster, Inc.
1230 Avenue of the Americas
New York, NY 10020, U.S.A.

For information about custom editions, special sales and premium and corporate purchases,
please contact Centennial Media at contact@centennialmedia.com.

Manufactured in Singapore

10 9 8 7 6 5 4 3 2 1

Publishers & Co-Founders Ben Harris, Sebastian Raatz
Editorial Director Annabel Vered
Creative Director Jessica Power
Executive Editor Janet Giovanelli
Deputy Editors Ron Kelly, Alyssa Shaffer
Design Director Martin Elfers
Art Directors Olga Jakim,
Natali Suasnavas, Joseph Ulatowski
Copy/Production Patty Carroll, Angela Taormina
Assistant Art Director Jaclyn Loney
Photo Editor Jennifer Veiga
Production Manager Paul Rodina
Production Assistant Alyssa Swiderski
Editorial Assistant Tiana Schippa
Sales & Marketing Jeremy Nurnberg